WORTHY WINS

POINTING YOUR LIFE TOWARD
WHAT MATTERS MOST

JOHN OLINGER

WORTHY WINS
Pointing Your Life Toward What Matters Most

Copyright © 2025 by John Olinger

Disclaimer: This book has been published for the purpose of providing the reader with general information on its subject matter. The author and the publisher believe the information to be accurate and authoritative at the time of publication. The book is sold with the understanding that neither the author nor the publisher is providing professional advice, and the reader should not rely upon this book as such. Every situation is different, and professional advice (whether psychological, legal, financial, tax, or otherwise) should only be obtained from a professional licensed in your jurisdiction who has knowledge of the specific facts and circumstances.

Scripture taken from *The Holy Bible, English Standard Version.* Copyright © 2000; 2001 by Crossway Bibles, a division of Good News Publishers. Used by permission. All rights reserved.

Interior Layout and Design by Stephanie Anderson
Book Cover Design by Michael Nagin

ISBNs:
979-8-89165-216-3 *Paperback*
979-8-89165-217-0 *Hardback*
979-8-89165-215-6 *E-book*

Published by:
Gordon Publishing
GordonPublishing.com

GORDON
PUBLISHING

To Erin, Jude, Kai, and Asher: You bring me joy, inspiration, and challenge. Your support in this endeavor is immeasurable. Loving y'all will always be worth it.

To my Dad: Thank you for modeling the pursuit of Worthy Wins in the way you laid down your life for me. You showed me what really *matters.*

CONTENTS

FOREWORD

WHEN I WORK with professional and college coaches, there is a unifying truth about those who are the best: They each have done the work to objectively define success for themselves and their teams. Yes, it's about winning games. But real success involves more than just wins and losses. Those best coaches realize that winning isn't just about what you accomplish. Focusing strictly on the outcomes is a short-sighted approach.

Coaches—and people—who take a long-term approach to winning consider the end goals they want to achieve and the relationships that must be created, cultivated, and maintained to do so. They have extreme clarity about what matters most because that is the starting point of success.

When I met John last year, it was obvious he had that same clarity. He had just completed a decade in marketing at Nike—a company that is all about winning. And much of his career had been spent working with some of the best athletes in the world, including three years leading global marketing for Kobe Bryant. He had been a part of and witnessed greatness firsthand, but it was his clarity about winning that drew me in.

John's personal story, combined with his professional journey at Nike, led him to see success differently than most people see it. Specifically, he talked about the reality that not every win we achieve in life is actually worthwhile, even more so, that we are at risk of getting to the end of our lives and realizing we won at things that weren't the most important.

I believe each of us has a purpose. But we are in a fight with confusion about what really matters. *Worthy Wins* is an antidote to the confusion. At a time when we have more options to engage with than ever, we need clarity about what is most important in our lives. We must decide what is worthy, and if it's worthy, then it's worth our focus and fight to make it happen and ultimately win. A big part of the winning process is the story we tell and the strategic plan we create, and there is no one on the planet better than John to help us with this process and planning.

If you want to unlock a new level of clarity about what is most important to you, build a plan to go after it, and then take action to truly win in your life, read this book. John's story and wisdom will provide you a chance to recalibrate success, move confidently forward, and seek out Worthy Wins in your own life. You will be encouraged and challenged to make the most of your time on this planet.

You will be better for it.
Your relationships will be stronger for it.
And in the end, all your effort will have been worth it.

JON GORDON
Seventeen-time best-selling author of
The Energy Bus and
The Power of Positive Leadership

INTRODUCTION

*Our problem is that this world does not
teach us to pay attention to what matters.*
JOHN ORTBERG

WHAT MATTERS?
On October 5, 2022, I stood naked in front of a full room of my coworkers at Nike.

Not literally naked, *obviously*.

But I was about to bare my soul with them—to share what *really* mattered to me.

This was two days before I was going to hand in my badge and walk away from an amazing career at Nike.

I had asked my boss for the opportunity to take over his staff meeting to reflect on my decade-long journey at Nike and Jordan Brand. Specifically, I wanted to talk about the wins and losses of my journey and how they might be helpful to my teammates as they moved forward in their careers as Nike employees. I wanted to give something back as I said goodbye to a company that had given me so much.

There were both good friends and literal strangers in the room, but no one knew the whole story of why I was walking away from a dream job. No one had experienced what I'd gone through during the previous two years. And none of them had any idea about the insane forty-day prayer journey that had flipped my world upside down two years earlier.

So, over the course of an hour, I peeled back the layers of my life and my heart. Though I had plenty to be proud of—from working closely with global icons like Kobe Bryant to game-changing takeovers that allowed kids to literally take Michael Jordan's game-winning shots for themselves—this was not a presentation about my greatest hits.

I wanted to share something more important than my wins.

In a setting normally reserved for business and marketing discussions, I chose to vulnerably bare my soul about the losses along the way.

What were my losses? While there were plenty of difficult moments in the work itself, the reality was that, at Nike, you don't take too many losses. It's not easy work, but either you figure out how to win at what you're responsible for or you don't stick around for too long.

This makes sense, given the starting point for Nike. In Greek mythology, Nike is the goddess of victory. The name (and thus the company) was literally built with winning in mind.

Secondly, in *Shoe Dog*, Nike cofounder Phil Knight drops this truth bomb about both himself and Nike: "Whatever happened, I just didn't want to lose. Losing was death."[1]

So, the only option at Nike was to win—at the work.

That meant that the losses I remembered from my journey weren't about the work.

My biggest losses were outside of work. So, as I shared, I reflected on the times I had missed out on key moments—including the Christmas I forgot to get my wife a present. (More on that later.)

I shared three questions with my soon-to-be-former team-mates that day that I had been wrestling with during my later years at Nike:

Can I win in my career without losing outside of work?

Can I win outside of work without losing in my career?

Can I win in my career *and* outside of work?

While at times it seemed impossible, I told them that day that it was, in fact, *possible.*

Not to boast, but I was living proof. I wanted them to know it was possible. There is hope for people who want to win in all the other areas of their lives, not just work.

I knew this because I was walking away on my terms, having won as a whole individual who was still following Jesus, with an intact marriage and family, along with having been successful in the work itself.

That was winning for me. Wholeness. My work took a lot, but it didn't take the things that mattered *most* to me.

I had won at the proverbial Hunger Games of Nike and corporate America.

And I won because I had learned a secret during my time at Nike. The secret was actually the most important thing I learned over my decade at Nike, and I wanted to share it with the team as I prepared to walk away. I wanted them to know this secret because it changed everything for me. So I told them my big secret about winning—and I'll tell you, too.

The only way to truly win—at work or outside of it or both—is to get extremely clear about what it means to win.

It sounds so simple and easy. And *obvious*, right?

If I'm not clear about what it means to win, then someone else will define it for me.

But we live in a world where we are being pushed and pulled and told what matters.

We're all just doing the best we can to survive amidst challenges and trials and children and injustice—and a million other things. We want to live good lives and have enough of what we need.

And all of that means it's easy to get confused or lose sight of what's most important. Of what it means to truly win.

Later in my presentation that day, I pulled up the quote from John Ortberg that I included at the beginning of this section because it illustrates the reality that we are all facing.

When you're going full-throttle in your career combined with all the chaos of just surviving life—your spouse, family, friends, fun, an ever-changing world—it's difficult to discern what matters.

In those times, what matters is surviving.

But I don't believe we were made to *just* survive.

We were created to have bigger and better ambitions than a life of just "making it."

Yet, discerning what matters can be confusing, whether or not we're in the midst of the *swirl of survival* (which I'll dive into more in chapter 9).

The truth is things that matter according to the world may not actually matter the most to me or you.

As I finished my presentation—and my career at Nike—I asked each person to take the time to ponder what matters most because that is the starting point of truly winning.

I wanted them to win on their last day at Nike, whether it came in one year or thirty years. I wanted them to have the same opportunity as me: to walk away whole.

I want the same for you. And it starts with the same question: What matters to *you*?

Over the course of my life and my journey at Nike, I've often found it hard to answer that question. There are a lot of things that matter to me.

In fact, everything matters to me. Every person. Every opportunity.

I want to—and have tried to—do it all.

But anyone who has been through a traumatic experience where death was near, whether their own or that of a loved one, will tell you that there is an extreme focus that comes in those moments.

The things that really matter become extremely clear when death is near. Shortly after Steve Jobs, the founder of Apple, had recovered from a rare form of cancer, he addressed the graduating class at Stanford University and emphasized this point: "Remembering that I'll be dead soon is the most important tool I've ever encountered to help me make the big choices in life."[2]

Psychologist Rollo May wrote about the clarity and benefit of associating with death: "The confronting of death gives the most positive reality to life itself. It makes the individual existence real, absolute, and concrete. Death is, in other words, the one fact of my life which is not relative but absolute, and my awareness of this gives my existence and what I do each hour an absolute quality."[3]

Being close to death makes us realize the value of life.

I know this firsthand. I write this to you from the point of view of an adult orphan—that is, an adult whose parents have both died. My mom passed away when I was eleven after a long battle with breast cancer. And my dad, who I'll share more about in the chapters to come, had a very strange accident that ultimately took his life when I was in my thirties. Both experiences—and the trauma that came with them—have shaped my life and my story immensely.

I'm not sharing this for pity, or to compare my life with others who have had it much harder. Plenty of others have had worse trauma than me. Yet there's no escaping the pending reality of death.

The reality is that, in the end, we will all eventually find ourselves near death, with the passing away of those we love and the end of our own lives.

That may sound grim, but it actually creates opportunity and urgency with how we live now.

Because of my mom's death when I was in elementary school, I've long sensed this undercurrent of life being finite—of death being nearer than it seems. Her passing woke me up to the reality that life was *short*—and that I didn't want to waste it.

But I wasn't totally sure what that meant.

I wrestled with that idea for much of my adult life without ever taking the time to get super clear about it.

Then my dad's death—more than twenty-five years after my mom passed away—blew up my life, and I couldn't ignore the nudges any longer.

In the aftermath of his death, I made a declaration to myself. That declaration is the reason I'm now writing this book:

I want to win where it matters.

Making that kind of declaration came at a cost for me. It meant I couldn't ignore the question any longer. The question that I started with at the beginning.

What matters *to me*?

Looking back, from the very beginning of my exploration of that question, my goal has been to win where it *really* matters to me. I'm talking about the important stuff—the lifelong, meaningful relationships and accomplishments.

The things that are most deserving of my limited time, energy, and attention.

The truth is that I want all the wins. But the reality is that I can win *almost* anywhere, but I can't win *everywhere*.

I cannot get all the wins.

So, if I can't get them all, then I want to be clear—I want to win where it's *worthy*.

According to Dictionary.com, *worthy* means: "Deserving of one's time, attention, or interest."[4] Those are the kinds of wins I want.

I want as many of my wins as possible to be Worthy Wins.

That's obviously the title of this book, and it's really a new way of categorizing the most important accomplishments I'm pursuing.

Worthy Wins are the wins that will matter at the end of my life. They are what I will look back on and say, "That was worth it."

What I've found is that they are a combination of the most meaningful relationships and accomplishments in your life. When your life is over, you want to be able to look back and see that the areas of your life where you invested and had success were the ones that mattered *most*. Those are the Worthy Wins.

Worthy Wins are long-term oriented, but they require your short-term attention.

They will be measured and celebrated at the end of your life, but they are reflective of what you invest your time, energy, and attention into today.

And that brings me to an important term we'll use a lot in this book: *TEA*, which is an acronym I use for time, energy, and attention.

We all have limited time on this earth, but time isn't the only thing in our lives that's finite, and it's not the only thing we need to invest to achieve our Worthy Wins. We also have to be willing to give our energy and attention—both limited resources as well—to the areas of our lives that matter most. We all have limited TEA, so it's imperative we use it in ways that lead toward Worthy Wins.

Ultimately, everyone has to make choices about what matters to them, and what actually matters to us is revealed by how we spend our TEA.

What I've seen in my own life is that, often, the worthy places are not the places I choose to spend my TEA. I'm prone to use my TEA to win in places that won't matter to me at the end of my life.

And because my TEA is limited, I must acknowledge the tradeoff: I'm inherently prone to lose in places that *will* matter to me at the end of my life when I've spent my TEA on other, less worthy aims.

This brings me to the risk that I know I face—and that I believe every single person faces: What if I get to the end of my life and I've won at things that do *not* actually matter?

What if I spend my TEA to win at things that are not most important to me?

From my journey at Nike, I know that's the risk I'm facing.

Pastor and author John Mark Comer says, "It's incredibly easy to waste our lives."[5] Yet, I feel the same today as I felt after my mom died: I do not want to waste my life. Now I'm just more aware of how easy it is to do so.

Since you've picked up this book, I believe you don't want to waste your life either.

I've written this book for multiple groups of people. First, for myself—to remember what is most important on my journey to win where it's worthy. And second, for my friends—both my literal friends who started on this writing journey with me three years ago *and* the people who are just like my friends. I've seen three specific types of my friends gravitate toward my writing during this time.

Maybe you are reading this because you're already cranking along on your journey through life. Things are going well, and you're feeling whole. You are thriving, but you are always looking for ways to get better. You want more tips, tweaks, hacks, and anything else that can help you do even better.

Or maybe you're the opposite, and life is difficult right now. The swirl of survival is real, and you feel like there's no hope— that you are stuck in a place that's mediocre at best, and that is how things will be forever. That you'll never be whole as long as things are the way they are. While it might feel that way, I've been through the mud of life, and there is hope. Even amidst challenging times, Worthy Wins are within reach.

Or you may be someone who would say life is good, but it feels like something is missing. It feels like your success isn't quite filling your tank up like it used to. You may need a refresher on what success looks like and what tweaks might be needed to help you go after it.

Regardless of where you're at in your life right now or what prompted you to pick up this book, I'm honored and grateful you're here.

This book is not about building complex systems or frameworks or about devising a million-step plan. I'm writing to make your pursuit of Worthy Wins *simple*. You need clarity about the most important targets and a plan to go after them. That's it.

You'll find in the pages that follow that I'm going to talk about Jesus and the Bible. My life has been forever altered by my faith journey of becoming a literal follower of Jesus, and there is wisdom to be shared and expounded on from that journey. Regardless of your faith background, you're welcome here, and you will find this to be a safe place for pursuing Worthy Wins together.

I'll finish here by telling you the same thing I told my coworkers during that last presentation at Nike:

My aim is to help you get more wins and take fewer losses.

Specifically, I want to help you win where it's worthy.

Let's go.

PART ONE

WINS AND
LOSSES

CHAPTER 1

FORTY DAYS

THE YEAR 2020.

I don't know about you, but it started with so much optimism for me.

I was in a literal dream job: Global Brand Director for Kobe Bryant at Nike. Our young family (four-year-old, two-year-old, and two-month-old) was thriving even as I sought to juggle my work and my family life. On top of that, we were living in Portland, surrounded by dear friends, and, importantly, my dad was only a short forty-five-minute drive away.

Life was good.

But it didn't take long for the year—and many good things in my life—to start crumbling.

Sunday, January 26, was the initial turning point, though there were more tough times to come for me and for us all.

It was supposed to be a normal Sunday, or at least as normal as they get when you have three kids under five cooped up inside on a rainy winter day in Oregon.

My wife had just stepped out for a workout class, and I was in the process of getting our two-month-old son down for a nap. As I burped him, I felt my pocket vibrate.

And then it vibrated again. And again. And again.

Finally, with my son passed out on my shoulder, I pulled my phone from my pocket. It showed a few missed calls and texts from my coworkers—definitely unusual for a Sunday morning.

I was still sitting in his rocking chair when I opened the first text. It was a screenshot of a tweet from TMZ.

Kobe Bryant had died in a helicopter accident.

No way.

Couldn't be true, right? *Right*?

The texts and calls kept coming for the next few hours. Everyone was hoping and praying that the reports weren't true.

Unfortunately, as we all know now, it was true. And it got worse—Kobe's thirteen-year-old daughter Gianna and seven other people had also been killed in the crash.

It was an absolute tragedy that sent shockwaves through the sports world. Kobe wasn't just one of the best players in NBA history—he was one of the most beloved, fascinating, and celebrated athletes to ever play the game. It was a massive loss on so many levels to so many people.

And for me personally, this tragedy had significant ramifications on my working world.

As we tried to come to grips with the tragedy, we also had to start spinning up a response. This was unprecedented. Nike had never lost a signature athlete at such a young age. We wanted (and needed) to plan something to celebrate Kobe's legacy, but we had to hit the right tone, celebrating Kobe without seeming like we were trying to capitalize on his life or his accident in any way.

In the immediate aftermath, the team created a few simple marketing stories. After the dust had settled, we landed on a bigger concept called Mamba Week to celebrate Kobe's legacy more officially and thoroughly. This ended up being one of the most fulfilling projects—if not *the* most—I've ever been a part of. It became the pinnacle of my work at Nike. (More about that later.)

Then, in March 2020, as we all know too well, the whole world turned upside down. The conversation around COVID started picking up, and it wasn't long before everyone at Nike (along with much of the rest of the world) was working from home. I remember saying goodbye to my coworkers, thinking we'd be back together in a few weeks or a month at most. Turns out I couldn't have been more wrong. (Nike's campus ended up being officially closed for twenty-six months.) That meant working from home became my new normal, and our family rhythm completely changed as my wife, Erin, and I juggled work responsibilities with energetic young kids.

I know I'm not alone in that. I'm sure, as it was for us, that it was *hard* for you.

The challenges of 2020 continued for me a few months later, in June, when Nike made a potentially life-altering announcement for my family and me—they were planning a gigantic reorganization of the business.

Translation: People were going to lose their jobs.

This meant for me—and for all my Nike colleagues—that my job *might* be at risk. There was no way of knowing whether my role would be safe, and there was no firm timeline on when to expect updates. All we knew was that they were going to be starting the reorg process and that any of us could be out of a job at any time. I'm generally an optimist, and I believed that I was contributing at a high level through my work at Nike. Even as I sat in the uncertainty waiting, I never really feared that my job would be gone.

And even in the moments I wondered and started to worry about the what-ifs, I had my faith and my experience to lean on.

This wasn't the first time I had been pitted with an uncertain and seemingly dire announcement.

I still remember driving north on Interstate 5 toward Portland as a ten-year-old when my dad shared a troubling announcement with me, the kind of announcement no parent wants to give: My mom had an advanced form of breast cancer.

She was going to be starting chemotherapy and a series of other treatments.

Obviously, that was shocking and disruptive for me. It was my first real experience with wondering and worrying about an uncertain situation.

And, unfortunately, even as my mom battled, the treatments were not enough to stop the cancer from killing her.

So, as an eleven-year-old, I found out that it was possible for a worst-case scenario to actually come true.

Yet, in the midst of mourning, I also found that the difficult moments are not necessarily fatal.

There can be opportunities for good even in the darkest of days.

While I was sad, God showed up for me in big ways in the aftermath of my mom's death. That foundational experience so many years before gave me confidence as I faced uncertainty at Nike. I believed that, however things played out with my job, God had the ability to help make good of the outcome.

He can make *all* things good.

When the reorg officially started, the announcements came in waves. The layoffs started with the most senior team members. Then, several weeks would go by before another announcement. My team hadn't been directly impacted in the early stages, and I was deeply immersed in leading the work for Mamba Week.

There wasn't time for wondering and worrying about things I did *not* control.

When Mamba Week came, it went incredibly well. We centered

the celebration of Kobe's legacy around two significant days: August 23, Kobe's birthday, and August 24, which was "Kobe Day" in Los Angeles—a combination of the two numbers Kobe wore in his career, 8 and 24. We created a short film for the celebration (aptly titled *Better*). The film centered on Kobe's passionate call to action for us all to become the best versions of ourselves by getting better day after day after day. That was Mamba Mentality in a nutshell. And it was the greatest legacy Kobe left the world. The film reached more than a *billion* people in the first week alone. I couldn't have been prouder of the work our team did.

In the midst of the trying nature of the situation, this was a pinnacle moment for me and my career. This is why I came to work at Nike: I wanted to impact people with powerful storytelling that could inspire them to act. And it literally felt like the opportunities to do that couldn't get any better than what we just did.

By this time, I still had five weeks of unused paternity leave to take from when our youngest son was born. Coming off Mamba Week was a great opportunity for me to lean in with my family while *not* having to juggle work as well. We were six months into COVID at this point, and Erin and I had been at home the whole time with big work projects on both of our plates in the midst of caring for our awesome, stir-crazy young boys. If you had kids at home during the early COVID days, you know exactly what this looked like—lots of great family time, extra time with the kids, but almost no time for Erin and me to spend by ourselves, just the two of us.

We had been in survival mode. There wasn't a lot of time to just *be* together.

Thankfully, Erin and I got some unexpected one-on-one time a few weeks later. We had been asked to co-officiate a wedding in central Oregon, and we had planned to make a family trip out of it during my paternity leave. But when the time came for the wedding, there were wildfires in the area—no one was staying overnight. So, we decided to make it an adults-only day trip instead.

We asked a friend to come stay with our kids for the day, and we hit the road for the wedding. Two four-hour drives, just the two of us.

It was the first real breather we'd had from parenting as a couple in six months.

As we were driving, Erin asked me what turned out to be a life-altering question for our family: "Have you thought about the possibility of moving east?"

Erin's family lived in Florida, and we had discussed the possibility of moving in that direction a few times before, but there was *always* a project or opportunity that I was really excited about leaning into at Nike. So, to this point in time, I hadn't been ready to leave the company, nor had working remotely from outside of Portland been an option.

But on this day, her question landed differently. The year 2020 had made it clear to me that life wasn't as simple as it had been before.

My priorities were under renovation.

All the COVID craziness at home with our kids made being closer to Erin's family really appealing. I was also, for the first time, in a place of true uncertainty around my future at Nike.

The wondering and worrying were *real*.

Maybe I'd still have a job in a year. Or, maybe I'd be out of a job in two weeks.

And on top of all of that, the Kobe work I'd just finished was like a mountaintop experience to me. From a work standpoint, would there ever be anything that could beat getting to celebrate Kobe's legacy?

It didn't seem like it. And that, too, had given me reason to consider a change.

So, I looked back at her and said, "You know what? I'm open to it."

Erin gazed back at me with a look of surprise and curiosity, given my previous answers.

After she took a moment to process, she asked me, "Are you scared of leaving Nike?"

Surprisingly, that was an easy question for me to answer. "I'm actually not," I said, "If this is the end, then I've had a great run, and I'm really grateful. I'm coming off Mamba Week, which is the exact type of work I came to Nike to do. So, if my time at Nike is done, I'm really okay with it."

"Well," she said, "is there anything that you *are* scared of?"

This time, I didn't need to pause to answer. "I'm scared of leaving my dad."

As I mentioned earlier, my dad and my stepmom lived about forty-five minutes south of us. We hadn't seen them much during COVID because he was older (seventy-four), and both of them were doing their best to stay healthy. Before the pandemic, we had seen them fairly often, but COVID changed things.

Yet, I was his only biological child. Us leaving Oregon would be tough on him—and me.

I knew he'd be supportive if we decided to move, but I hated the idea of having to tell him we were moving further away—especially all the way across the country.

For someone like me who wants to have it all—the best of all the worlds—this was tough. The reality was I couldn't have it all.

I wanted to stay close to my dad, and I had a great job at Nike.

I also saw lots of value in our family moving closer to Erin's parents. I didn't feel like I had clarity on what to do, but we began processing the question of what mattered most to our family. We had two paths in front of us: stay in Oregon or head east.

Which one was best?

Which one was most *worthy?*

Erin and I kept talking about it as we drove, and ultimately, we decided we needed to pray. Like, *really* pray, not just say we were going to pray about it. But intentionally commit to praying.

So, we agreed to pray for forty days to see how God might move during that time.

There were two things we knew: This was a *big* decision, and a time period of forty days had biblical significance. We also felt like it would be enough time to make sure that whatever decision we made, we were making it intentionally and inviting God to join us in it.

We kicked off the prayer journey that day as we drove, hungry with anticipation for what God might reveal to us over the next forty days.

We had no idea what was about to flip our world upside down.

THE PRAYER JOURNEY

WE ANTICIPATED THAT we'd have clarity after forty days. But it took much less time for our lives to change in a big way. And it wasn't the change either of us expected.

At eight thirty in the morning on day five of our prayer journey, I saw my phone ringing. My stepmom was calling, which was pretty unusual, but our house was in a moment of total chaos.

Life was chaos in general at that point because of the age of our kids, but mornings, in particular, were not a great time for me to take a phone call. So, I silenced my phone and made a mental note to call her back later.

But then Erin stopped me. "I'm not sure why she's calling," she said. "But I think you're supposed to answer it."

So, I quickly answered the phone before it went to voicemail. "Hello?"

From the first word she said, I could hear the fear in my stepmom's voice. "John, it's your dad," she said. "He's had an accident. He slipped and fell in a parking lot. An ambulance is taking him to the hospital. I don't really know anything else, but I'm headed to the hospital right now, and I wanted to let you know."

I sat there stunned in the midst of the chaos.

Really? A fall in a parking lot? Not good, obviously, but probably not life-threatening. I forced myself to believe he'd be okay, that they'd get him to the hospital, take care of him, and he'd recover just fine. What else could I do?

A few hours later, my stepmom called with news that was worse than I expected. "John, your dad's in the ICU," she said. "The accident was pretty serious. They're running a bunch of tests on him. Unfortunately, only one family member is allowed to be here at a time, so I'll keep you posted on everything. I'm really sorry you can't come."

So I waited a day. Then another, and another, and another. Finally, going on five days of my dad being in the ICU, I had my first opportunity to go and be with him. After clearing all the COVID protocols, I made it into the hospital and did what pretty much everyone has to do in these situations: I sat there and just stared at him.

I felt so helpless.

So powerless.

I had so many questions. How was he really doing? What was his prognosis? Was he going to be fine soon, or was he on the verge of dying? Should we keep him here, or should we try to get him to a higher-ranked hospital in Portland?

He perked up a few hours into my being there, and he did seem to be making progress. Yet, a lot of my questions didn't have clear answers—or timelines.

This wasn't how Erin and I imagined the beginning of our prayer journey going. The only thing we could do in the midst of the wondering and worrying was to *keep* praying—for my dad, for his healing, and for God to continue to guide us on what all of this meant for our family. So that's what we did.

Days went by, and my dad's condition was all over the place. He'd improve, and then he'd regress. He was intubated upon his initial entry into the ICU. Then he made enough progress to come off the intubator. But one night, he was struggling badly to breathe, and they had to intubate him again.

I knew this was *not* good. We'd been told that if he had to be put on intubation three times, there was a good chance he'd never come off. So a second intubation meant that things were getting serious—and options were getting more limited.

At this point, I was trading off with my stepmom and going to the hospital every other day. We were doing the best we could to advocate for him, to try to make sure we made the best decisions for him. But it was hard. There were so many questions and still not a lot of answers from the doctors.

As we waited, hoping and praying for my dad to improve, Erin and I reached day thirty-nine of our prayer journey. My dad's situation had obviously moved front and center for me, but things hadn't stopped churning at Nike. The reorg was still in full swing, and there had just been a wave of layoffs at the level above me that resulted in five of my previous six bosses being let go in one day. I still hadn't heard anything about my job, but with the way things had been going, I was guessing I'd hear something soon.

I was right.

On day thirty-nine, I got an email from Nike informing me that I had a meeting the next morning with my boss and someone from HR. If you've worked in a corporate environment, you know what that means: I was about to find out my fate. I might walk out of that meeting with my current job, a brand-new job, or no job at all.

And so, on day forty of our prayer journey—not day thirty-nine, not day forty-one, but day forty—I signed onto a Zoom meeting with my boss and the HR rep.

As soon as I was admitted into the meeting, my boss smiled at me. "Look, John," he said. "We think you're doing great work. We're excited to have you here at Nike, and we've got an important role for you to take on. It'll be a change, but we think you'll be great."

"Okay," I said. "Tell me more."

"We'd like you to be the Global Brand Director for Men's Running," he said.

"Okay," I said. And then I paused.

I knew it was a great job—one that lots of people would love to have. But I'd been thinking for a while that the next thing I wanted to do was to lead a team of people, and it wasn't clear if this job would allow that. I was ready to invest my time in people more than projects.

"Will I have direct reports in this role?" I asked.

"No," my boss replied. "Not at this time."

"Do you think that's something I'd have the potential for in the near future?" I asked.

"John, you're right there," he said. "You need just another year or two, and then I think it could be a real possibility."

Another year or two? That answer was murky at best. Even more, it was confusing. I'd had multiple roles in the past where I was directly responsible for leading people—I wanted *more* of that. I wanted to help more people succeed in their careers at Nike. Why couldn't I have that responsibility in this role? As I was advancing my career and experience, why would they take away responsibility?

Turns out it wasn't a "me" issue—it was an organizational change aimed at flattening the company's hierarchy. It just happened to affect me. But it left me with a feeling of discomfort and uncertainty.

I felt like I'd been preparing to lead *more* people, not take a step backward. I didn't want to waste another two years of my life (if not more) waiting for something that was *really* valuable to me.

Yet this was a take-it-or-leave-it offer—I was either going to accept the job they offered me or walk away from Nike. And even though I was disappointed, I knew I was lucky to be offered a job at all, let alone a good job like this one. Accepting the job would allow us to keep things stable for our family and give me the chance to continue spending a lot of time at the hospital with my dad.

So I said yes.

But that didn't mean that our forty-day prayer journey was over.

INFLECTION POINTS

ERIN AND I finally got a chance to talk that night after the kids went to bed. We never would have guessed forty days ago that we'd be talking to each other with my dad in the hospital. We knew there had been uncertainty at Nike, but we didn't know that we'd have such fresh clarity on my new role or that it was going to keep me from doing the kind of people-focused work that I was feeling drawn to. It truly had been a journey—of praying but also of wondering and worrying.

Erin asked me what I felt like God had said to me over the past forty days. "I feel like he's telling us that he trusts us," I said. "That there are going to be challenges no matter what, but we can choose which way we want to go, and he'll go with us."

Erin said she felt the same way. We knew that we couldn't make any final decisions with my dad in the hospital, but we both felt that when the time was right, God was offering us the freedom to choose what was most important for our family.

Our story had reached an inflection point. The possibility of moving east to be closer to Erin's family had hovered over us for years, but now we were staring it directly in the face.

And as nice as it would have been for God to just write us an answer in the clouds, he was handing the decision back to us.

So many times in my life when I've looked to God for guidance on a decision, I've found myself asking him to send me a sign—to give me some kind of direction and make it so clear that I can't miss it.

And sometimes he might do that.

More often, though, what I've found is that God is less concerned with the path I choose and more concerned with how I'm following him as I walk that path.

This runs counter to what some of us who grew up going to church might have been taught—that God has one singular plan for your life, and if you aren't carefully trying to discern where exactly He's telling you to go, you might pick the wrong direction and ruin everything.

But all of that ignores one of the most basic truths I know about God: that he's always with me. No matter what path I'm on, he's always by my side—in the good, bad, and ugly. He may have been offering Erin and me freedom to make the choice that we wanted to make, but he was right there with us in the uncertainty, stirring the desires of our hearts.

It would take faith to stay in Oregon, and it would take faith to move east.

I believe there's a lot of value in asking God for direction and discernment. I believe he shapes our hearts and minds as we invite him into the journey with us. And in this case, one of the ways He was shaping our hearts and minds was by offering us this push—and this freedom—to choose.

On behalf of our family, we had to decide what was best. What was right.

What was *worthy*.

CHAPTER 2

BIG MOVES

OVER THE NEXT couple of weeks, I continued going to the hospital every other day to be with my dad. With the reorg still ongoing at Nike, my workload was relatively light. So I was grateful to have a bit more flexibility to spend time with him. With so much uncertainty around his condition, I wanted to be there as much as I possibly could.

Unfortunately, it wasn't long before we began to notice a change in my dad.

The occupational therapists would visit each day, full of joy and optimism. But his ability to do the rehab that would be critical to his life outside the hospital was actually regressing. Scarier than that, he was becoming less and less himself, to the point that one day, when I walked into his room, he asked, "Who's that?"

Sigh.

His doctors and therapists were trying everything, but it was like his body and brain just could not get on the same page. They eventually diagnosed him with a serious form of sleep apnea that essentially caused his brain to tell his body when he was sleeping that he was not going to wake up.

Every time he dozed off to sleep, he'd jolt awake, literally thinking that he wasn't going to be able to take his next breath.

I'm talking *big* jolts.

Shoot straight up in bed in *panic* jolts.

He couldn't express himself in these moments, but the sound of his groan and the look on his face said enough.

Anyone who has been in these situations where recovery is needed knows that if you can't sleep, you can't recover. That meant my dad was quickly running out of options.

We could intubate him again, which would technically keep him alive, but his doctors strongly recommended against it because it wouldn't change his prognosis. They suspected that he had an undiagnosed brain stem injury, but they weren't able to do an MRI to confirm that because they couldn't sedate him. They told us how sorry they were, but there was *nothing* left they could do to help him.

I didn't want to wave the white flag on my dad's life, but none of us wanted to prolong his suffering. And it was clear he was suffering.

We had fought hard for him, prayed hard for him, given him everything we possibly could.

He had fought too.

But I didn't want to put him through any more suffering. The downward progression of his sleep—getting fifteen to thirty-minute stints at best before the apnea jolted him awake—made it clear to me that the doctors were right. He wasn't going to recover. My stepmom and I knew it was time. We told the hospital staff to start comfort care as soon as possible.

My dad died less than twenty-four hours later.

We said our goodbyes, and I was grateful I'd had time with him in the hospital to say all the things I wanted to say. We weren't able to have a full funeral for him because of COVID restrictions, but we had an outdoor burial service a few weeks later surrounded by twelve friends and family members in Oregon's cold December air.

In the days after my dad's death, lots of thoughts and feelings were swirling through my head and heart. I had never expected to lose him so young or for it to happen so suddenly. Even though I was glad he wasn't suffering, I was *sad*.

But I realized that what I was grieving most was time: *intentional* moments together.

Another breakfast. More conversations about my mom. The chance to watch a Blazers game together. One more round of golf.

We had done all these things, but if I had known that time was going to run out, I would have done them more consistently, and I wouldn't have taken them for granted. I thought we had more time.

But I was wrong.

I'll forever want my dad back. But this experience would also permanently change the way I looked at my own life. It became a very real, tangible reminder: I don't get to decide when my own time is up.

And that means I don't know how much time I have left.

My dad was seventy-four when he died, and I was thirty-seven.

Important truth: If I lived exactly as long as he did, my life was already 50 percent done at that moment. *Halfway* over.

I started asking myself questions. If my life was half over, how should that change the way I think about living? Who are the most important people in my life, and how do I make sure my decisions reflect that? When I look back at the end of my life, what do I want to see? What purpose was I put on this earth to live for?

What *Really* Matters?

Losing my dad was the most difficult experience of my adult life. But it changed me in positive ways, too, ways that I hope would be a tribute to my dad. His death gave me two things in particular: a sense of urgency about my time and a clarity of focus on what was most important. This fueled me to make more of my own life, and to focus my time, energy, and attention—my TEA—on the people and things that matter most.

THE CHOICE

SHORTLY AFTER MY dad's burial service, Erin and I went to breakfast together, just the two of us. This gave us a chance to talk after the dust had settled a bit. She asked how I was feeling after everything that had happened.

My answer came easily. "Time is short," I said. "I feel like we're supposed to move to Florida to be closer to your parents. They love our kids, they're healthy, and they want to be in the mix. I think that's what we're supposed to do."

"Are you sure?" she asked.

I nodded. "I don't want us to look back and wish we would have spent more time close to your family. I love working at Nike, but it's not as important to me as making the most of the time we have with family. I think we should go."

This was a *big* moment. We had never talked about moving to Florida specifically. It had always been about moving east to get closer to her family. Maybe Nashville or Raleigh, but not Florida. But at this time, after this series of events—this journey of praying, grieving, and processing—Florida felt like the best place for us.

Erin was surprised by that, but she ultimately agreed to go

on the journey. Over the course of the next six months, we sold our house, packed up our kids, said goodbye to our dear friends in Oregon (whom we still miss greatly), and moved our lives to St. Augustine, Florida.

This didn't mean there was a "right" or "wrong" choice.

If we'd have stayed in Oregon, our family still could have had a great life. But to us, this was a moment to lean into our family's relationship priorities. We knew what mattered most to us wasn't just about "what" but also about "who." And for us in this season, that additional "who" was Erin's family.

It wasn't clear what this decision meant for my career at Nike. We were planting a stake in the ground that being close to family meant more to us than my ability to work at Nike headquarters in Oregon. Yet Nike's offices were still closed at this point. Everyone was working remotely. So, other than aligning my workday with Pacific time (*not* fun with young kids, by the way), I could work from St. Augustine just as easily as I could from Oregon.

But I also wasn't being naive. I knew the corporate world wasn't going to stay fully remote forever. And I knew that when we chose to move to Florida, there was a good chance it would eventually mean the end of my career at Nike.

So I started knocking on other doors. And while there weren't a ton of organizations the size of Nike within striking distance of St. Augustine, I was still able to find a few opportunities that seemed promising. But each one ended in disappointment. I kept looking and knocking, and in the meantime, I continued working at Nike.

My leaders and my team at Nike knew that we moved to Florida. I had been transparent with them about our family's plan from the beginning—specifically, that there was no plan to return to Oregon. But I was also clear with them that I was committed to continuing in my role with excellence. As long as I was part of the Nike team, I was going to continue doing the best work I possibly could. But it became evident that my relocation was lingering in the back of everyone's mind. Although I didn't commit to moving back when the office reopened, I assured them that I was still all in.

Decision day was coming, though. Three different times, Nike tried to reopen the office, only to postpone for a few months because of COVID spikes. It was only a matter of time before they pushed the "go" button and began asking everyone to return.

So I kept seeking out opportunities, and eventually, my search led me to a job opportunity at Disney. I was encouraged right away when I saw that the role could be located in either Florida or New York—that told me remote work might be a possibility. So I applied and went through the interview process, and eventually, they offered me the job.

It was a good job with significant benefits, but I had been clear with them that a big part of the reason I applied for this job was because of the remote-work potential. We lived two hours' driving distance from Disney on a good day, and I did *not* plan on moving to Orlando or commuting on a regular basis.

Then, as they were finalizing the job offer, there was a strong point of clarification.

"We know you're looking for remote work, John, and we support that," the recruiter told me. "We just want you to be really clear on what you're signing. If you accept, you're agreeing that this job is officially three days a week in the office."

Whoa.

This caught me off guard. "Is there flexibility?" I asked. "Can we officially change that language to say something different?"

"We'll be flexible with you," she said. "Don't worry. We understand where you're coming from. But formally in the contract, we want to be explicitly clear that this role is three days a week in the office."

I asked if I could have the weekend to think about it, and they agreed.

Later that day, I told Erin about Disney's offer, and over the weekend, we had the chance to talk about it. "It's great that they want you," she said. "But do you really want *this* job?"

I thought about it for a moment. "Well, no," I said.

"Then why would you take it?" she asked.

"Well, because I know I need *a* job. Nike's campus is going to reopen in a couple of weeks," I said. "They've made it clear that everyone needs to be in the office in Oregon three days a week. And that obviously doesn't work with us living in Florida. So taking this job at Disney would provide for our needs and compensate me well. In that sense, it's a good job."

"Sure," she said. "But I know you. If you really wanted this job, then you'd be willing to figure out a way to make it work." She paused for a moment before she delivered that most important question: "Is what this job requires *worth it* to you?"

I knew Erin was right. She was asking me if I wanted the job.

But what she was really asking me was: Is this job really worthy of your limited TEA?

If it were, then I could (and should) figure out how to make it work. But if not, then saying yes to this job would mean saying no to other things—the very things we had just prioritized by moving to Florida.

This job was not worth what I'd have to give up for it—either staying in Orlando three nights a week or commuting four hours (at best) back and forth each office day. It wasn't worth the time and energy it would take from me or the time it would take away from being with my family. So, I reached back out to Disney, thanked them for the offer, and turned them down.

As I did so, the countdown was on for me. Nike was moving closer and closer to opening the office back up—for real this time. I had about three weeks before I'd be expected to return to the office. I had told my leaders I was committed to the job, but I knew the conversation was coming soon where I'd have to finally give them an answer on whether I was willing to come back to work in person. I was as all in as I could be from across the country.

But I knew they were going to want more.

LEAVING NIKE

ON MY FIRST day back in the office, I boarded a 6:00 a.m. cross-country flight from Jacksonville to Portland. The flight landed at PDX at 9:00 a.m., and by 10:30 a.m., I was sitting in my first meeting with my boss, Drew, having the inevitable conversation.

After some pleasantries, he cut to the chase. "John, we've had a couple conversations about you being all in," he said. "But it's going to be hard to continue doing that from across the country. So, what's your plan?"

"I'm still all in," I said. "I'm still committed. But I'm not ready to decide about my future yet."

He was understanding and also clear. "We are going to need to know soon," Drew said. "We want you here, but working long-distance isn't a long-term solution."

"I understand," I told him. "I know I'm due a sabbatical in about a month, and I'd like to use that time to come to a final decision."

He acknowledged my desire, and we left the conversation there for the time being.

Over the next few weeks, I traveled back and forth between Florida and Oregon, splitting time between my new home state and the state that had been home for so long. Suddenly, I was seeing less of Erin and the kids than I had for a long time, even back when we had lived in Oregon and I was going into the office every day.

I had asked for time to consider my decision during my sabbatical. But in my heart, I already knew the answer.

We had moved to Florida for one reason: family. I was choosing time with family over my job at Nike. Were we going to change our minds and move back just because Nike was reopening the office? Was I going to commit to flying back and forth every week and end up spending less time with family than if we'd just stayed in Oregon in the first place?

If I wanted to win in the areas that Erin and I had said mattered most to us in this season—the areas most worthy of our TEA—I knew what I had to do.

I made one last trip to Nike before my sabbatical. Just like the first trip, I got off the plane and headed straight to campus to discuss my future and my fate at Nike with Drew. This time, he cut to the chase quickly. "I know we said we were going to discuss this after your sabbatical," he said. "But we need to know what your plan is sooner than that. If we need to fill your position, we need to start looking. So, tell me where you guys are at. Are you going to move back to Oregon?"

"I love being a part of this organization," I said. "I've loved all of my time at Nike. And I don't have any plans to quit. But we also don't have any plans to move back. That's my answer."

"Okay," he said. "I understand. But if you're not moving back, we think it would be best if you resigned."

I had prepared myself to hear those words. I knew something like this was probably coming. And I didn't *have to* agree to it—I could have refused and put the onus on them to fire me if they wanted me to leave. But I had valued my time at Nike so much. They had treated me and my family well. And more than anything, I desired to finish well, to maintain the good relationships I'd built, and to leave with the same integrity I'd tried to maintain the entire time I'd worked there.

"I understand," I said. "And yes—I'm willing to work with you guys on that."

So before I returned to Florida for my sabbatical, my leaders and I landed a date in October—a full four months later—for me to officially depart the company. In some ways, it was like picking a retirement date, except that I was only thirty-nine and still had to keep working.

When I got on the plane to head back home that week, it was officially official: my time at Nike was ending.

And I had chosen what was best for my family over what was the best job opportunity.

I had declared that I wanted to win where it was *worthy*.

When I returned from my sabbatical ten weeks later, my leaders had already filled my position with my friend Kate, who had been working under me—the exact person I would have picked if the decision had been up to me. It was the best transition I possibly could have hoped for. I stayed on for three more weeks, helping the team prepare for my departure and doing whatever I could to add value.

Prior to my sabbatical, I had asked my vice president, Rami, if I could take over his staff meeting during my last week. This was an unusual request for a departing employee, especially because I didn't know exactly what I was going to talk about. I just knew I wanted to encourage the team. Thankfully, even sight unseen on the content, Rami agreed to give me the full hour to pour into them.

Over the previous nine months, I had begun writing a weekly newsletter to a group of my friends about winning where it's worthy (which eventually led to the idea of Worthy Wins). This was a subject that had become important and personal to me and had driven a lot of the decisions I'd made since my dad died, starting with our family's decision to move to Florida. And now it was leading me to say goodbye to Nike.

As I prepared to stand in front of my coworkers at that final staff meeting, I couldn't shake the feeling that I was supposed to share with them about the same thing—what I had learned from my time at Nike and Jordan Brand about winning in the most important places in our lives—the worthy places.

On the day of the meeting, we gathered the team together in our area of the Serena Williams building. As I plugged my laptop into the monitor, I looked out toward the group. There were dear friends I'd known since my first day at Nike, and there were literal strangers who were probably wondering what kind of meeting they were walking into. Regardless of our relationship prior to that day, they were about to get to know me and my story in a new way.

I started by sharing about why I was walking away from Nike: my dad. The move. The fork in the road to decide if I was coming back.

There were tears—from me and from the team.

This was the most vulnerable presentation I had ever made at Nike, but I felt compelled to share with my soon-to-be former teammates.

There was too much at stake for them.

It's the same reason I'm sharing all of this with you in this book—there's so much at stake for us all.

Most people are so deep in their work—even amazing, life-giving work—that they don't take the time to count the cost of it all.

I know that because I've been there.

Deeeeep in the work.

Pushing and pushing and pushing to bring greatness and inspiration to life. Until finally something—usually related to the people I love the most—breaks.

Psychologists like Dr. Janna Koretz say that these types of situations represent a perfect storm of enmeshment (overattachment to our work) combined with burnout (exactly what it sounds like and what we all know it to be).[6] When there are tangible incentives—promotions, increased compensation, prominence, relationships—tied to overinvesting the amount of TEA we give to our work, it creates a significant challenge to fight against this cycle. Enmeshment sets in, and then burnout follows.

And that cycle is repetitive.

I had been caught up in it plenty of times along my journey at the Swoosh. I was leaving Nike whole, but that was only because I had done the work to recalibrate and put the pieces back in the right order.

I wasn't more special than anyone else. But I had a perspective that most other people don't have at my age.

Both my parents were dead.

It was crystal clear for me that the end will come—and that I didn't want to have wasted my limited time, energy, and attention.

My TEA *will* run out.

And it's possible that it will be sooner than I hope or think.

There are lyrics from a song in *Hamilton* that have stuck with me since the first time I heard them. The first act of the musical closes out with a song called "Non-Stop." In it, the cast members question Alexander Hamilton about how he does what he does and if he knows something they don't know. The song builds as Aaron Burr leads the ensemble with a series of questions for Hamilton and ultimately culminates with them asking him if he's running out of time.

Did Hamilton know his life would be short? Or was he just living like it?

He never formally answers the question for the cast, but that doesn't matter.

Either way, it was clear he was living and working with extreme urgency because he knew his time—and thus, his TEA— was limited. So, he was approaching his life to make sure he got the most important things done (though you could argue he didn't always accurately choose which things were most important).

What I've found is that it's usually not until death comes near— personally or for a loved one—that you realize how short life is.

And when that happens, you also realize that there is more to life than winning at work.

My journey with my dad made it clear to me: I wanted to win in the places that mattered most—the *worthy* places—because I had felt the pain of losing in those places and with the people who mattered most to me.

So what I wanted to share with my teammates that day—and with you as you read this—was about perspective.

About how we're *all* running out of time.

Hamilton knew it. I know it now.

When my time runs out, I want to have won more often than not in the places that matter most. But often, the wins at work (and at Nike, for me, there were plenty of wins) come at the expense of losing in other places that *really* matter to me.

But it doesn't have to be that way.

I wanted the team to learn from my journey. So, as I continued sharing, I didn't tell them about my best projects at Nike. I told them about my most painful losses.

And none of them had to do with the work itself.

They were born out of losing sight of what mattered most to me.

I had been blinded by my pursuit of winning at Nike.

All these losses affected *people*. Starting with me and then unavoidably overflowing onto the people I loved most. My wife, my kids, and my friends.

Nonetheless, I told the group that even though I experienced pain and losses along the way, I felt like I was walking away from Nike, having won. I was walking away on *my* terms: as a whole individual who was still following Jesus, with an intact marriage and family to show for it—along with the success of the work itself. I told them that my hope for them was that by figuring out what mattered most to them in their lives, they too could walk away from Nike whole, whether in the near future or decades down the road. My hope was that they would achieve more Worthy Wins and suffer fewer painful losses.

When the hour was over, there were hugs.

And more tears.

And thank-yous—both from my longtime friends and the people who began the meeting as strangers. It was clear that the message had resonated and affirmed to me that I wasn't alone in my desire.

No one wants to win at work but lose where it's worthy.

A few days later, on October 7, 2022, I turned in my badge and walked out of Nike for the last time. And a bit more than a week thereafter, on October 16, we hosted a celebration of life for my dad in the town in Oregon where he'd grown up, the first proper celebration of his life we'd been able to have with a large group of people. I got to hear new stories about him, what he was like growing up, how the people who'd known him remembered him. It was a kind of closure that I hadn't experienced since his death. It was a gift.

A NEW CHAPTER

TWO MAJOR CHAPTERS of my life had closed in less than ten days.

On my own volition, I left Nike—a dream job and company—where I'd been working for more than a decade. And we were able to properly say goodbye to my dad and celebrate his life.

We had been living in Florida for a year and a half by this point, but it finally felt like the Oregon chapter of our lives had closed. And the next chapter of my life was starting—one that God had been setting up for a while.

Even while I was at Nike, God had been dropping a trail of breadcrumbs, pointing me in the direction of the consulting work I do now. A few months earlier, a friend had asked me to speak to a group of nonprofit leaders about storytelling and communication, which led to a consulting session with one of the attendees, which led to some longer-term consulting work, which opened my mind up to the possibilities that might be available to me in the future. It started small, but more opportunities began coming my way that made me stop and think that this small thing could possibly become a bigger thing.

But I was scared.

The idea of giving up the security of a steady paycheck was frightening. Yet becoming a consultant full-time was the rubber meeting the road in my journey of pursuing Worthy Wins. At this point, I had spent a lot of time talking to other people about this subject. Was I willing to put it into practice myself? What did winning look like for me in this new chapter of life? What had I been saying was most important to me all along?

Upon reflection, the answer was simple: I wanted to prioritize time with family, and I wanted to use my work to invest in other people. Could we have decided to move back to Oregon, kept my job at Nike, and held onto that financial security and consistency?

For sure. But at this point in my journey, how I defined winning had changed.

The wins of climbing the ladder at Nike were no longer the most important wins for me. Committing to full-time consulting work was scary in some ways, but it also represented the best chance for me to win where it mattered *most*.

The questions I've had to answer on my journey are the same ones we all face in our lives:

Where do I *most* want to win?

In a world filled with endless opportunities, what's most important?

What people and accomplishments are most worthy of my TEA?

These questions are the starting point. If we take the time to answer them, they can help us make sure that we're winning in the areas of our lives that matter most. I believe it's some of the most significant work any of us can do in our lives.

These last two chapters have been about my journey to win where it's worthy. Now, in the rest of this book, I'd like to share how you can join me in the same pursuit—but on your own terms. We'll talk about what Worthy Wins are and how to identify them in your life. Then we'll dive into how to create a plan to pursue them consistently and deal with the inevitable challenges you'll face along the way.

Making a declaration that you want to pursue Worthy Wins can change the way you live your life.

I know because it's changed mine.

PART TWO

WHY WINNING
MATTERS

CHAPTER 3

WINNING IS SUBJECTIVE

WHEN KOBE, GIANNA, and the other seven passengers were killed in that tragic accident, I was one of the only people at Nike who actually had "Kobe" in their job title. I'd been working with Kobe for more than two years in that role, getting to know him as a person, an athlete, and a businessman. I was blessed with the opportunity to spend enough time around him to have clarity about what mattered to him and what drove him.

As I mentioned in chapter 1, Nike had never experienced a tragedy like what happened to Kobe, someone who was a big part of their brand and was so beloved around the world. After the accident, the wheels started turning immediately within Nike. My team had always been focused on Kobe, but suddenly, there were multiple groups around the company who (understandably) wanted to be a part of honoring his legacy. So many people at Nike cared deeply about Kobe, his message, and what he meant to the world, and they wanted to help make sure we responded in the right way.

In the days following Kobe's passing, there were mixed emotions around Nike, but the passion for honoring him was incredible. Lots of people wanted to devote their expertise to making sure Nike did right by Kobe and his legacy. It was amazing and humbling to see.

But alongside all those positives came a more challenging reality: When many people care about a project, there are going to be *a lot* of ideas on what the project should look like.

Even though I was the Global Marketing Director for Kobe, in a matrix organization like Nike, there's often shared ownership in a situation like this because different people "own" different pieces of the work that needs to be done.

There were *a lot* of different points of view about what it should look like for us to celebrate Kobe and his legacy, and it was often unclear who was "in charge." Especially when senior leaders with big titles got involved.

But what was clear was that if we didn't align on what success looked like—what it meant for all of us to win on this project—we were at risk of losing. Without that alignment, we would be vulnerable to using our resources—both our budget and our TEA—in the wrong places.

If we were going to have unity in our message across the globe, with all the teams throughout Nike speaking and pulling in the same direction, we needed clarity about our target.

**There *has to be* clarity
to create consistency.**

Without clarity of our aim, it was possible—maybe even inevitable—that we would be inconsistent in our actions as a company. Yet the overall goal was obvious: honor Kobe and his legacy.

But if we were going to truly succeed, we knew we had to be

explicitly clear from the start on what success actually looked like for us.

We had to agree on a definition of what it would mean to win.

And to me, there was no doubt what Kobe cared about most.

He was spending his TEA on passing his philosophy—Mamba Mentality—to the next generation. It was clear that was a Worthy Win for him after retiring from the NBA. So as we sought to align all the teams to focus on the same target, we decided that on this project, that's what winning would look like for us, too.

My team made a declaration: The objective of this project is to continue Kobe's work of passing down Mamba Mentality to the next generation of athletes, with a specific emphasis on Gen Z girls. (And at Nike, "athletes" meant everyone—one of the guiding principles was "if you have a body, you are an athlete.")

Getting clear about our target required explicitly defining what it meant to win. And once we did that, figuring out our next steps suddenly became *much* easier.

Even though there were people working on the project literally all over the world, we were all aligned on the same target. That gave us a shared purpose. No matter a person's role on the team or at what time they joined the project, the aim was clear. In every single slide deck we created for the project, we included the exact same slide with a clear representation of the objective: pass Mamba Mentality on to the next generation with an emphasis on Gen Z girls.

This became both our North Star and our filter, the thing that drove all the decisions that we made on the project. It gave us guard rails to align how we should (and shouldn't) spend our resources and TEA to celebrate Kobe's legacy. And it led the Kobe project and what ultimately came out of it—Mamba Week—to be some of the most successful, fulfilling work I got to be a part of during my time at Nike.

DEFINING YOUR WINS

At one point in Amazon's documentary series *All or Nothing: Arsenal*, the manager of Arsenal, Mikel Arteta, flips an interview segment back on the production team to make a point.

He puts a picture on his monitor—one of those images that can be seen multiple ways. In this case, some people on the production crew see a duck, and some see a rabbit. It can be interpreted either way.

But those differing answers represent the problem for Mikel and Arsenal as they pursue becoming a more successful team. He says this:

> *This is the most difficult thing in a football club…and in the process we are in right now, it's even harder. My only aim is that everyone sees the duck or the rabbit. Because if you see the duck and I see the rabbit, then we are going in different directions. But that thing we are starting to get in line…where we all see the duck.*[7]

That sentiment perfectly represents the challenges we face in our lives, both personally and professionally. Some pictures can be interpreted subjectively. People can see things differently, and even I can be divided about the true picture of success within myself. Yet like Mikel says, the aim is for us to have unity and clarity about what the picture is.

Winning must be objective in order to move with consistency.

On any significant project, if the people involved have different points of view on what a successful outcome should be, the likelihood of success is low. You're going to be all over the place as a group, unsure of how to get where you're going because you haven't defined where you want to go in the first place. But if you've defined what winning looks like, you'll have a clear destination, which will give you clarity as you plan the steps that will get you there.

This applied to my work on Mamba Week (and so many other projects) at Nike. But it applies to life, too. The "life" part is obviously a much more individual experience—you don't have a company full of stakeholders with different opinions on what it looks like for you to succeed in your own life. But *personally* defining what winning looks like is just as important. If you don't decide what it means for you, you may get to the end without ever knowing whether you won or not.

Or even worse, you may realize you *lost* at things that were *truly* important to you.

This brings me to the most important takeaway about success that I learned at Nike.

Remember: In Greek mythology, Nike is literally the goddess of victory. And as Nike cofounder Phil Knight said, "Losing is death."[8]

I learned a lot about victory at Nike.

But in the midst, no one ever taught me what I'm about to tell you. I only learned it as a result of the journey.

And it's something I believe we all need to be clear about.

Winning is *subjective.*

That means each person defines it in a *different* way.

Just like in the beginning around the work for Kobe. Everyone at Nike had a different idea of what it meant to celebrate Kobe's legacy. It's the same with our lives. Everyone has a different idea of what it means to succeed in their own life.

That means I can't tell *you* in this book specifically what it should look like to win in *your* life.

And honestly, that's a beautiful thing.

Everyone gets the chance to uniquely identify what victory looks like for themselves. Once you define your own target, then you get the opportunity to go out and pursue it.

But with that freedom comes a responsibility: If we don't define the terms, we won't win.

When you establish for yourself what winning truly means, it will drive the decisions you make, and those decisions will move you closer to what you want to be true of your life. But if you don't, your decisions—and the trajectory of your life—will be scattered.

Will that lead to the outcome you *most* want? Maybe, but probably not.

It's incredibly difficult to hit a target that hasn't been defined.

Also, it's important to say that your definition of winning can change based on the season of life you're in. There may be outcomes you chase your whole life and others that change with time. And while the most important wins to define are the over-arching ones that you want to be true about your entire life, you will likely have season-specific aims you're striving for with your loved ones, at work, and beyond.

For me, especially when I was early in my career, success largely meant advancing to the next level—getting the next promotion, making more money, and gaining more responsibility. It drove the decisions I made, and it motivated me in the work that I did. But along the way, I always felt like there was something more that went into my formula for "success."

And then, in January of 2019, my definition of success changed in a crystal clear way. I had just completed leading the biggest project of my career to that point. Inspired by the infamous Air Mag and its powered lace system from the movie *Back to the Future*, we had launched the Nike Adapt BB, the world's first basketball shoe with a motor inside of it.

This was the future, literally.

Power laces. (Yes, shoes that tied *themselves*.)

Bluetooth connectivity.

Lights that could change colors.

Worn in real NBA and WNBA games by some of the best up-and-coming young players in basketball like Jayson Tatum, Luka Dončić, A'ja Wilson, and Breanna Stewart. It was *insane*.

For some of my teammates involved in the design of the shoe, this had been years—even decades—of work. For me, the journey had been about a year and a half, but it had been a heavy lift the whole way. It was a company-wide, global initiative that required immense teamwork and coordination. Still, by all accounts, it was a successful launch. A win for the company and for me personally.

The week after the shoe launched, my boss, Craig, asked me a question that I was totally unprepared for, "What do you want to do *next*?"

I was caught off guard. The honest answer was that I hadn't thought about it one bit. The future was the furthest thing from my mind because I had been *deep* in the Nike Adapt BB work. (Remember how earlier I told you what it was like to get lost in the work? That was me during this project.)

I needed time to actually think about it. I asked Craig for a week.

What became clear in that week of reflection was that my definition of success had changed. It was no longer just about leading big, impactful projects so that I could get promoted. I had just led a gigantic project, which was wonderful. But I realized I wanted to have a greater impact—for the company and myself. Rather than focusing solely on my own career and accomplishments, I wanted to spend more of my time directly investing in other people. I wanted to take the things I'd learned and share them with others to help them grow and succeed in their own lives and careers.

The question from my boss was an ignition moment.

Questions can do that.

Famed motivator Tony Robbins says this: "Quality questions create a quality life. Successful people ask better questions, and as a result, they get better answers."[9]

We must ask ourselves—or be asked by others—about what really matters to us.

A good question can completely alter the course of our lives.

For me, Craig's question made it clear that my definition of winning had changed. And it turned out that was the beginning of my journey toward the consulting work I do now.

And why I've written this book.

That's the power of good questions.

I want to pause for a moment and clarify my use of the word "winning." It's a word I like to use, as you might have figured out by this point. But the kind of winning I'm talking about in this book doesn't have to mean you're competing against someone else. It doesn't have to mean that you're trying to be the best in an industry or make the most money or impact the most people. Though it might mean one of those things for *you*.

That's why it's so important to understand that winning is subjective.

Every single person has the opportunity to individually decide what their definition of winning is.

Sure, for some people, their ideal outcome might mean being the very best at what they do professionally or vocationally. The greatest to *ever* do something.

Maybe that's you.

But maybe it's not.

Maybe for you, it means finding ways to serve people and make a difference in the world or in your community. Maybe your aim is to be the kind of intentional parent you want to be or to be a dedicated friend to others. Maybe you're like Erin and me when we moved to Florida, and success means protecting and prioritizing time with your family.

Ironically, winning doesn't need to be comparative or competitive. It just needs to be true to what's most important to *you* and what *you* want to be true about *your* life.

But there has to be clarity about the target you're aiming at. Otherwise, it's easy to get distracted—and even discouraged.

A few years back, I found myself at a retreat with fifty amazing men from all over the country, most of whom I didn't know previously. This was an incredibly accomplished group, and they were all doing impactful things in the world.

On the first night, as each person shared a bit of their story, I found myself sinking into a place of comparison. I felt like an imposter. "Am I good enough to be a part of this group?" I asked myself. "How can I compete with these entrepreneurs? Do I have anything to offer these guys?"

These questions kept flooding my mind, and I really felt inadequate during that first evening of the retreat. I couldn't shake the feeling that I did *not* belong.

I woke up early the next morning, feeling refreshed from a good night's sleep after a long day of travel, and I took some time to be alone and reflect. What would it look like *for me* to win in the midst of the retreat with these guys? Was it being able to stack up with them from a business perspective, to feel like I could compete on their level? Or was it something else?

It didn't take me long to realize that I had the wrong perspective.

First of all, I hadn't come to this retreat to compete or try to prove myself. I had come to learn, to reflect, and to spend time with God. Comparing myself to these other men had never been part of my plan.

Second, I had come to this retreat to be *myself*, not someone else. I didn't need to be just like anyone else there or use them as a standard to measure myself. I needed to be me. And that meant defining what success meant for *me* at this retreat, not what it meant for someone else.

So, I decided that I would commit to *serving* rather than competing with the other guys at this retreat. This allowed me to move forward with a clearly defined idea of how I would know whether or not I had won when it was over: listening, learning, asking questions, and pouring into the men around me. This was how I operated normally. How I operated in my day-to-day life at Nike.

Clarifying my definition of a successful retreat changed my mindset, and instead of leaving with a feeling of insignificance, I walked away refreshed and recharged. And I was able to help a handful of different guys in their work and personal lives.

It's just one small example. But it's a great encapsulation of how defining winning for myself dramatically changed my situation for the better, even for the short period of time I was at this retreat. It impacted the actions I took, the decisions I made, and, ultimately, the outcome I left with.

I recently spoke with a good friend of mine who found himself on the other end of the spectrum. My friend is an author and speaker, and he made the decision this year to put out a podcast episode and an email *every day* for the whole year. Literally. From January 1 to December 31.

When I checked in with him a few weeks into January, he shared with me that things seemed to be going well, but not perfectly. He wasn't sure if his work was accomplishing as much as it could, but he didn't know what he needed to do to make it better.

So, I challenged him to more intentionally define what success would look like for him on this year-long project. "You're near the end of January," I said. "At the end of February, how will you know if the month has been successful? You're putting in a lot of work, so if you're going to make it worthwhile, you need to have an answer."

My friend responded with lots of ideas on what he wanted to accomplish in February: books he wanted to sell, speaking engagements he wanted to land, a contract he wanted to finalize.

But he never actually answered my question.

He defined several goals he had for February but never articulated how his chosen strategy—extreme content creation—laddered up to any of them.

If my friend had taken the time to define the ideal outcome *before* choosing a strategy, would he ultimately have chosen to create emails and podcasts?

Probably.

But would he have seen the same benefit from creating three pieces of content each week instead of a new piece *every day*? And would that have opened up time that he could have used to make the content better and pursue other wins in his career or his personal life? Almost definitely.

When I followed up with my friend to probe a bit deeper about how he was going to evaluate success on the daily emails he was sending, he admitted that he needed to look at some actual metrics rather than just measuring by putting out a piece of content each day. And when he looked at the metrics around growth, opens, and unsubscribes, the results were not positive.

He realized his definition of success wasn't actually about publishing content daily.

He needed to get more specific about success so that he could tailor—and, in this case, evolve—his strategy to set himself up to win.

KNOWING WHERE YOU'RE GOING

Last year, I was sitting on the runway at the Atlanta airport, and I snapped a picture out the window. There were Delta airplanes as far as I could see, one lined up after another. Literally fifty, even sixty airplanes. They all looked exactly the same from my vantage point. Yet, everyone who arrived at the airport was going to get in one of those planes, headed for some *specific* destination.

But none of those people were just showing up at the airport and saying, "Today, I think I'll get on the sixth plane down."

You don't show up at the airport and just hope you end up in the right spot. You're there because you have a specific destination in mind.

The planes look similar, but they're all going to different places. And there are people getting on each one of the planes—you can't just follow the crowd to determine which plane is best for you. The only reason you know which one to board is because you determined your destination before ever going to the airport.

We are all going *somewhere*— toward *some* destination.

At the end of your life, and at the end of this year, and at the end of this day, you will have arrived at a destination. The only way to make sure that destination is where you want to go is to get clear about it *before* you go. It's critical to determine what success looks like for *you*.

Because being victorious means different things to different people.

But one thing is true for all of us: You can't actually win if you don't first define what winning means.

REFLECTION QUESTIONS

As discussed in this chapter, questions help drive clarity. For the remaining chapters, I'll include some reflection questions at the end of each chapter that may be helpful for you to consider.

- Have you *explicitly* defined what it means to win in your life?

- Is there an area of your life where it may be helpful to get more clear on what it means to succeed?

- Think of a friend, family member, or someone else in your life. How does winning look different to you than it does to them?

CHAPTER 4

WINNING AT THE WRONG THINGS

IN THE YEAR prior to an Olympics, you'll find teams all over Nike working together to create consensus and alignment around the stories that will be the most important and impactful to lean into around the games. And that's exactly what was happening in 2019—we were in full buildup mode preparing for the 2020 Tokyo Olympics. (This was pre-COVID, so there hadn't been any talk of delaying the Olympics yet.) And collectively, we landed on a story that we all strongly believed in: *The Greatest Dynasty Ever.* (I'll call them the GDE going forward.)

Everyone talks about the Dream Team, the United States Men's Basketball Team that won gold in 1992. But the real story of the most dominant team at the Olympics over the past three decades had gone untold.

Enter the United States Women's Basketball Team.

The US Women were going into the 2020 Olympics seeking their seventh straight gold medal.

They hadn't even lost a game in the Olympics since 1992.

During their gold medal run, they were winning by an average of thirty points per game.

Now, *that* is a dynasty.

And two of the players on the 2020 team—Sue Bird and Diana Taurasi—would ultimately become the most decorated basketball Olympians ever with their fifth gold medals at the 2020 games. (Until Diana played again for Team USA in the 2024 Paris Olympics to collect her sixth gold medal.)

We knew that the GDE had the chance to capture people's attention, and we felt like it was a story that deserved to be told. People all over the company were excited about it. And we decided, in order to tell this story well, we needed to bring key members of the GDE to Nike World Headquarters (WHQ) to capture content that we could use for our marketing campaign around the team. We'd set the ladies up for a few awesome days in Oregon, complete with workouts, interviews, new shoe and apparel testing, and time to engage with employees on campus. And, importantly, we planned to let the cameras roll for every moment.

Needless to say, this was an organizational nightmare.

Many of the best ideas are.

To make our plan possible, we were going to need *a lot* of internal alignment. First, we had to get buy-in from decision-makers all over the company. It was a bit challenging to get all the respective leaders across Nike on board, but we got it done. That was only the beginning, though, as we then needed at least eight different internal teams to come together to make the experience special and seamless.

There was one complication for me.

I was leading the project, but we were about to have our third son. When the day came for the birth, I handed the project off to a couple of my teammates and headed off on paternity leave.

Three weeks later, just after Thanksgiving, I jumped back into the sprint to get ready to welcome the ladies to WHQ the first week of January. Because Nike shuts down for two weeks at the end of December, we essentially had three weeks to prepare, get everyone on the same page, and make sure every detail was dialed in to make the absolute most of their time at Nike.

It was a *big* lift.

When I was at work, I was completely immersed in preparation.

And at home, we were in the midst of adjusting to having a new baby and now playing zone defense with (against?) the three kids.

I was trying to pull my weight at work, deliver excellence on this project, help out with the kids, be a good dad—I was trying to do it *all*.

The days and weeks sped by, and eventually, the holidays arrived. We had finished the prep work we needed to do at Nike, and we were ready for the ladies of the GDE to arrive at the beginning of January.

I was proud of the work we'd done.

As the leader of the project, it felt like we had won. We were set up for success and ready to tell an amazing story. But I realized pretty quickly that this win at work came at the cost of another, much more important win.

When Christmas Eve arrived, I was hit with a heartbreaking realization: I didn't have a meaningful gift for Erin for Christmas. Over the last three weeks, I had put so much of my focus on the project at work that I'd let finding Erin a gift slip through the cracks.

And it was too late to find something meaningful.

I was *stuck*.

I knew Erin would be hurt. And even worse, there was no excuse.

Then came the proverbial walk of shame.

I was so embarrassed having to explain to Erin what happened. She was gracious, but my intuition was correct—she was also very hurt. She rightly felt like I hadn't made her a priority. My actions had communicated that she wasn't worthy of the small amount of TEA it would take to get her a meaningful gift for Christmas.

Erin wasn't looking for a gift that was monumental, fancy, or expensive.

It wasn't about the gift itself at all.

She just wanted me to show her that I saw her as worthy of my TEA—that she mattered enough to me that I would prioritize her, even when life was crazy.

I wanted her to know she was worthy also. I truly did (and still do) value her, of course. I did not *intend* to forget about her.

It wasn't my goal to not buy her a Christmas gift. But I'd entered into my busy work season between Thanksgiving and Christmas without defining what mattered most to me during that time. So I worked hard on the project, and I won there. I worked hard at parenting, and I think I won there, too (as much as any new parent of a third child can, at least).

But in that time period, I hadn't gotten clear that winning in my marriage—making Erin truly feel like a priority—was worthy of my TEA. And as a result, I failed in the most important human relationship in my life.

I won, but not where it mattered most.

I won at the
wrong things.

Thankfully, I know I'm not alone in this problem.

In *The Good Life: Lessons from the World's Longest Scientific Study of Happiness*, Robert J. Waldinger and Marc Schulz write this hard truth: "Our brains, the most sophisticated and mysterious system in the known universe, often mislead us in our quest for lasting pleasure and satisfaction."[10]

What do the authors mean?

Our brains lead us to make decisions that are not the best for us. And I see this in myself in this situation.

I knew what was good for me—what mattered to me—and yet I failed miserably. In the midst of life and challenges and chaos and wanting to do well, it's easy to be misled. And Waldinger and Schulz remind us that it's our own brains often doing it to us.

THE MYTH OF INFINITE TIME

One of the challenges we face is knowing just how many different things we can do every day.

We live in a world of *endless* opportunities.

Technology and the internet have made nearly anything possible for us, and there are a million things out there that we could decide to spend our TEA on.

But, unfortunately, we do not live in a world of infinite time. We all get twenty-four hours each day, seven days each week, and a limited amount of time to live on this planet.

We can do almost *anything*.
But we can't do *everything*.

I mentioned earlier that when my dad passed away, I was half his age. It was a strange thing to process, an odd experience to truly realize for the first time that I might be halfway done with my life. Ever since my mom's death, I'd understood cognitively that life is short and that I shouldn't take it for granted. But my dad's passing was a wake-up call for me.

I could no longer act as if I'd have infinite time to do the most important things in life.

Most sales gurus would tell you that putting an expiration date on an offer is one of the most effective levers you can pull to get customers to buy in (both literally and figuratively). If a potential buyer feels like there's infinite time, they can always wait for later. But if they realize time is limited, they'll be pressed to identify their priorities and decide before time runs out.

That's how I tend to operate as well. When I don't have an expiring timeline, it's easy for me to let my focus drift. When it comes to things that are important but not urgent, I've been guilty of putting them off to the side and saying, "I'll get to that later." But as I've become more aware that my TEA is limited, I've gained a sense of urgency to choose wisely.

I've discovered that the *most* worthy places are not always the ones where I naturally choose to spend my TEA.

I'm prone to win in places that won't matter to me at the end of my life.

And because my time, energy, and attention are limited, I'm inherently prone to lose in places that *will* matter to me at the end of my life.

That's why intentionality is so important.

If we're going to win in those places that matter *most*, we have to intentionally determine what those places are. If we don't, we leave it to chance, all but guaranteeing that the places we win at the end of our lives won't be the ones that matter most. When we choose to pursue things that aren't actually the most important things to us, the opportunity cost is our own Worthy Wins. In those instances, we give up the things that are most important to pursue the things that aren't.

But if we are intentional—if we take the time to get clear on what it looks like to win where it matters most—then we can align our actions to those outcomes and make sure they happen.

We can use our limited TEA to achieve our most Worthy Wins.

SOLUTIONS START WITH PROBLEMS

Every marketing brief starts with a problem that needs to be solved for the consumer. And for good reason—any marketing that doesn't solve a problem for the consumer is just noise in a very noisy world.

When I was working in Nike Running, there was a simple problem we were trying to solve for one particular set of consumers: "How to run faster marathons."

We had solutions for their problem, including best-in-class shoes to help runners go faster. We also offered a lot of additional tools—inspirational stories, training plans, coaching content, and more—to support runners as they worked to improve their marathon times. We understood their problem, and that helped us to determine, as marketers, how we needed to communicate with them to help grow their awareness of the solutions we offered.

Two things are true here. First, our understanding of this consumer's problem was essential in helping us find the solutions that were right for them. And second, the solutions we were offering were not right for everyone. A consumer who was looking for more comfort and stability on the basketball court wouldn't benefit much from our communication about marathon running. But because we were clear about the problem we were trying to solve from the beginning, we were able to plan our communication in a way that solved our problem without getting bogged down with all the other problems that we *could* be solving.

Identifying the problem is the starting point to finding a solution.

It's true in marketing, and it's true when you're trying to determine the Worthy Wins you want to strive for in your life. Starting with the problem you're trying to solve is a great way to find clarity on defining what winning looks like for you.

We're all doing our best to live our lives well in the midst of the chaos that we face, but if we're not clear about what winning looks like for us, we'll end up succeeding at the wrong things—like when I won at work but didn't get Erin a Christmas present.

We're all at risk of spending our limited TEA in places that aren't actually the most important to us.

That's why, before we can achieve our Worthy Wins, we need to take the time to figure out what being victorious actually means.

If you're having a hard time determining what winning looks like in your life or a particular area or season of your life, here's a question I've found helpful: What do I want to be true about my life in a year that's not true right now?

Answering this question is like identifying the problem that exists in your own life, and it can help lead you to the solution you want to pursue. It can help in whatever area of your life you need clarity, whether it's broad or specific. What do you want to be true a year from now that's not currently true in your family? In your career? In your friendships? In your marriage?

You can lean on others to help you process this question, but ultimately, your answer has to be personal. Identifying the "problem" you want to solve in your life will give you clarity on what investments are most worthy of your TEA and what steps you should take to pursue the wins that matter most.

FOLLOWING THROUGH

This is really important to call out: We're all doing our best.

Almost everyone operates with good intentions, trying to make the most of what we have and where we are in life. Nobody steps into their marriage with the intention of being a bad partner. Nobody steps into parenthood with the goal of being a terrible mom or dad. Nobody walks into the first day of their new job determined to do so-so work.

No one is trying to win at things that *don't* matter.

And generally, even if we sometimes lack clarity in certain areas, deep down, we all understand the things that matter most in our lives.

But there's a big difference between *knowing* what's important and *doing* what's important.

Or, more specifically, taking the steps to follow through on what's most important.

If you had asked me that Christmas Eve whether making sure Erin felt valued was important, I would obviously have said yes. But when I was working on the Greatest Dynasty Ever project at Nike, I lost sight of that truth. I knew what was important, but I didn't follow through.

Can you think of a time when that's happened in your life? When you (probably unintentionally) prioritized *an* important thing but realized too late you had neglected the *most* important thing? It likely led to regret, maybe some hurt, possibly an apology.

Whatever example you're thinking of is a great reference to the difference between knowing what's important and following through. This isn't meant to be a guilt trip, and it doesn't make you a bad person—I'm as guilty of this as anyone.

The point is to further illustrate the reality we've been going back to for most of this chapter:

We have *infinite* opportunities but *limited* TEA.

There are lots of places where we could focus our TEA that are good. But to truly win where it's most worthy, we have to find the places that are best, identify how to prioritize them, and follow through.

WHAT WILL YOU CHOOSE?

When I visited Israel in 2008, it changed my life and my faith completely. It brought a new sense of realness to the things I'd been believing. Suddenly, I wasn't just reading about Jesus's disciples following Him—I was seeing the places they went together, walking the paths that they walked, understanding the tangible ways that they had to operate in order to do what Jesus was calling them to do.

In Matthew 4:18–22 (ESV), Jesus invites the men who would ultimately become His disciples to follow Him:

> While walking by the Sea of Galilee, he saw two brothers, Simon (who is called Peter) and Andrew his brother, casting a net into the sea, for they were fishermen. And he said to them, "Follow me, and I will make you fishers of men." Immediately they left their nets and followed him. And going on from there he saw two other brothers, James the son of Zebedee and John his brother, in the boat with Zebedee their father, mending their nets, and he called them. Immediately they left the boat and their father and followed him.[11]

The men Jesus called didn't just say, "Sounds good, Jesus. We're following you now. We'll just be here in our fishing boats, hanging out by the sea. We'll see you when we see you!"

Jesus meant for them to *literally* follow him.

And if they were going to do that, they had to *literally* act. His invitation wasn't a thought exercise for them—it required full commitment and follow-through.

This is true for us today too. We can have all the ideas in the world about what's important in our lives. We can even identify specific ways to pursue those things. But if we don't follow through, those thoughts will stay thoughts, and nothing in our lives will change.

It would be so much easier if we were just hardwired to do the right thing all the time. But that's simply not the reality for us as humans. Even if we know what's best for us, it's not always our natural instinct to do it. Some things will get prioritized, and others will fall by the wayside.

And make no mistake: Things *will* fall by the wayside in your life.

The only question is—which things? Which people?

Big question: With the way you're living *right now*, are you comfortable with what those things and people will be? Are they going to be the things that matter most to you, or less important things that you can let go of?

The apostle Paul put it this way in 1 Corinthians 9:24 (ESV): "Do you not know that in a race all the runners run, but only one receives the prize? So run that you may obtain it."[12]

We're all running, and we're all going to end up *somewhere*. But if we want to reach our Worthy Wins, we have to do more than just run. We have to run in a way that will lead us to the prize.

Opportunity is everywhere, but TEA is limited.

And every day, we get to demonstrate what is most valuable in our lives through the way we spend our time.

What we prioritize shows what we value, and it will ultimately determine whether we win in the right places—or the wrong ones.

REFLECTION QUESTIONS

Here are a few questions you can contemplate as you process this chapter.

- If an outside observer watched how you spent your time, would they say you're living like you know time is limited?

- Can you think of a time in your past when you let something that truly mattered to you fall by the wayside?

- What *specifically* do you want to be true of your life a year from now that's not currently true?

CHAPTER 5

WINNING WHERE IT'S WORTHY

LAST FALL, I was scheduled to fly from Jacksonville to Denver for a retreat. The day of the trip began like a normal travel morning for me: I left my house about two hours before departure time, got to security about an hour before my flight, and then walked up to the gate just before boarding was set to begin.

But that was where the normal part stopped.

Shortly after I arrived at the gate, someone from the airline announced there would be a "short" delay. The crowd let out a small groan, but it didn't seem like a big deal to most of us.

Until that short delay turned into a four-hour delay, which ultimately ended with us leaving *eight* hours after the scheduled departure.

Travel delays are the worst, right?

Wrong. Enter Jon Gordon.

Jon is an amazing, thoughtful human who also happens to be a world-renowned coach, speaker, and author. He is *legit*. And it turned out we were traveling to the same gathering and on the same (super delayed) flight to Denver.

Despite many mutual friends in common and living fairly close to each other, this was our first time connecting. We decided to make the most of the opportunity and sat down for lunch in the midst of the delay. Over our meal, we got to know each other better and shared stories about our lives. Jon is such an encouraging person, and he asked me to tell him more about my vision for this book.

I told him how I wanted to encourage people to win in the places in their lives that were most worthy of their time. And as he listened, Jon came up with a line that's stuck with me to this day:

"If it's worthy, it's worth it."

Worthy things are the ultimate things.

They're the accomplishments that, at the end of your life, will have been worth all the TEA that you spent on them. They are what the people you love most will talk about at your funeral. And Jon summed it up so well:

Worthy Wins are worth all the effort it takes to achieve them.

But let me state the obvious for us: This is hard!

If getting Worthy Wins were easy, we'd all be doing it already.

But the most important and meaningful things in life are hard to do. The fact that they're challenging is part of what makes them meaningful. Worthy Wins require something of us. They ask us to make a choice, to demonstrate their importance through our actions, and to say no to other things so we can say yes to them. Because the truth is that we can't say yes to everything.

Not everything can be worthy.

We continue to come back to one simple question: What do

we want to be true when we reach the end of our lives? What will we look back on as having been a worthy investment of our TEA? If we're clear on the answer to these questions, then we can start to figure out what winning where it's worthy looks like in our own lives.

Elon Musk is, to put it gently, a bit of a polarizing figure. You might love him, or you might hate him. But he said something about what mattered to him when he first bought Twitter (now X) that caught my attention. He made a declaration about what success would look like on the platform he now owned. Elon specifically said over and over that for "new Twitter," his goal was to maximize "unregretted user minutes."[13] He said this was the metric that mattered most for the platform's success—that of the time users spent on the site, they would regret as few of those minutes as possible. Simply put, he wanted people to feel that the time they spent on Twitter was worth it.

Isn't that what we all want at the end of our lives—to look back with as few regrets as possible?

We are all looking to maximize our unregretted user minutes.

But to do that, we have to take the time to identify *now* what that means for us because the reality is that our clock is ticking. (We need to get clear on what wins are most worthy in our lives.)

TIME UNCERTAINTY

There is a reality about time (and TEA) that constantly sits below the surface for me—one that's true for every single one of us: We don't know how much time we have left.

Do we have decades?

Years?

Less?

I'm not trying to be morbid, but I want to keep it real. None of us are guaranteed a certain number of years.

So that means there is a tension we are all wrestling with. And these three questions illustrate it:

- How do I make the most of the short term without ruining the long term?
- How do I wisely plan and prepare for the long term without missing out on the short term?
- How do I find the right mix between the short term and long term when I have no idea exactly how much time I have left?

If I knew exactly how much time I had left on this earth, then I could plan it out with precision. I could make perfect decisions to ensure that I'm spending my precious TEA in the ways I really want. I could find the exact right balance in my short- and long-term planning to win where it's worthy.

But the reality is that I have no idea how much time I have left on my personal clock. I may live for another sixty years, or I might get in a car accident tomorrow.

Obviously, I hope I live another sixty years, but that might not be my story. That might not be the way that God wants to use me on this planet.

So, that begs the question—how does God want to use me with however much time I have?

The ironic part about pursuing Worthy Wins in the short term is that it's built on being clear about what it means to have won at the end of my life.

But what I've found is that our culture tends to distort our view of success. That's why it's critical for us to declare both who and what is worthy.

WHO + WHAT

Our culture is adamant that winning is all about *what* we accomplish. But there is an underlying body of both art *and* science that's screaming for us to realize what winning in this life is truly all about: relationships.

Waldinger and Schulz speak to this in *The Good Life*: "The consistent signal that comes through after eighty-four years of study and hundreds of research papers, it is that one simple message: Positive relationships are essential to human well-being."[14]

While *what* we do has an impact on our lives, the one simple connecting thread across the whole eighty-four-year study is all about *who*. Despite our inability to comprehend it, who is actually more important than what.

Embracing the *what* is simpler and clearer because the *who* (a.k.a. our relationships—not the band) is complicated and ever-evolving. It's easier to focus on *what*, so that's where our brains draw us.

On top of that, as I mentioned above, the culture of our world is so heavily focused on *what* we do.

But just because our culture tells us something is best doesn't mean it's right.

The data illustrates this very point: We broadly, as humans, are terrible at knowing what is best for us. I pointed it out in chapter 4 when I talked about the way that I somehow decided to prioritize my work over getting my wife a Christmas present. Our amazing brains don't always point us in the right direction.

This makes me think about Paul's letter to the followers of Jesus in Rome. He was making a plea to them to live *differently* than the culture of Rome, which feels like a fitting reminder here as well: "Do not be conformed to this world, but be transformed by the renewal of your mind, that by testing you may discern what is the will of God, what is good and acceptable and perfect." [15]

We don't *have to* be like the rest of the world.

We can be transformed into something different in partnership with God. We can pursue true success that goes against our cultural norms.

But there's a distinction we must make in order to do so. And it comes down to the "where" in "winning where it's worthy."

What do I actually mean by "where"?

It would be easy to assume that where is all about *what* we accomplish. But in reality, it's a combination of who (our relationships) *and* what (our accomplishments).

So, for each of us to truly win where it's worthy, we need clarity on both the most important people we want to cultivate strong relationships with over the course of our lives *and* the meaningful accomplishments we want to go after.

In the end, our Worthy Wins will be a combination of who + what.

SCARCITY, SCOPE, AND PRIORITIZATION

And as much as I want all the wins, there are some limitations I have to acknowledge.

The truth is that we have more opportunities than we've ever had. The internet and technology have given us exposure and access to information and experiences that are never-ending. We live in a world of infinite possibilities but limited time. So, by definition, not everything can be worthy.

Not everything—or everyone—deserves your TEA.

Does that sound harsh? It's felt that way to me in the past, as someone who wants to win everywhere and with everyone. I'm not naturally great at saying no to things. And I really do love people. So the idea of labeling certain people in my life as unworthy feels wrong.

Let's clear that point up first. There are a few sticky truths about winning where it's worthy when it comes to people. First, determining our most Worthy Wins should almost always start with who, not what. We have to prioritize the *most* important people in our lives. But with people, just like with anything else, we can't do everything. We don't have unlimited TEA to invest in every single relationship in our lives. And that means, to say yes to some relationships, at some point, we're going to have to say no to others.

That doesn't mean you're required to cut anyone out of your life. And it doesn't mean you're viewing anyone as a lesser person or that you're *literally* labeling them as unworthy. All people are worthy of being loved, being cared for, having people in their lives who know them, understand them, and value them.

What you *are* saying when you make the decision to invest in some relationships is that those relationships are so valuable to you that you're willing to invest your TEA into them, even if it comes at the expense of other relationships. It's not an indication of anyone else's character or value. This is an act of love toward the most important people in your life.

Our relationships and every other part of our lives are subject to three realities: scarcity, scope, and prioritization. The more willing we are to accept that these are part of life for us and every other human on the planet, the more we'll be able to realistically identify our Worthy Wins and pursue them wholeheartedly.

Scarcity is a concept I've referred to over and over already: Our time, energy, and attention are scarce, *limited* resources. We all get twenty-four hours a day, and we have to spend some of those hours sleeping.

We're people, not machines.

And that means the amount of energy and attention we have is actually *significantly* less than the number of hours in the day.

A number of researchers have explored the limits of both physical energy and mental attention. While we can all acknowledge that even the best athletes in the world run out of energy after several hours, it's easier to think that we have *unlimited* mental attention and energy. Professor and author Cal Newport famously claims that our brains and bodies max out around four hours of deep work per day.[16] Doctor Andrew Huberman from Stanford University asserts that our best blocks of focused work expire after ninety minutes and then require defocused work to allow our brains to recover.[17]

To summarize, we have a lot less energy and attention than we have hours in a day.

Say it with me: We can do anything, but we can't do everything.

Scope is how scarcity plays out in our lives.

Even if we believe that every relationship is important and everything we do matters, because of time, energy, and attention scarcity, we can't win everywhere and with everyone. Even when you spread it as thin as you can, eventually, there's no butter left to spread. The scope of what we're capable of is *limited*.

Prioritization is what's required to win despite the realities of scarcity and scope. Because our TEA is scarce, and because we can't win everywhere and with everyone, we have to do the work of prioritizing what's most important.

When you lay it all out, it almost sounds like I'm stating the obvious.

Time is limited. Therefore, we can't do everything. Therefore, we should choose the things that are most important and do those things.

But just because it sounds simple doesn't mean it's easy.

This is *hard*.

Yet, doing this work is one of the most important things we could ever do.

Our ultimate goal is to be able to look back at the end of our lives and say that we spent our TEA in the places that mattered most—that we maximized our unregretted user minutes and stayed true to our priorities in how we chose to spend our limited resources.

And if we're going to do that, we first have to get clear on what those priorities are.

PAUSE OR BE PAUSED

If you want to win where it's worthy—to ensure you're investing in the right places—you have to be willing to do the upfront work. Your other option is to start traveling down the road, only to realize several miles in that you should have picked a different road to begin with. Either you can take the time up front to determine what your Worthy Wins are, or you can wait for the truth to catch up with you.

You can *choose* to pause now, or you can be *forced* to pause later.

I once worked with a consulting client who had big ambitions and was pushing to move fast. This client wanted to change the world. They wanted to grow a huge brand, build a massive business, and accomplish a lot of big goals. And there was nothing wrong with any of those things.

From my point of view, though, there was some upfront work that needed to be done first in order for this client to truly be successful. They had big, broad dreams. But they needed to get specific—to identify what Worthy Wins they wanted their business to deliver down the road.

So, I asked them: "Why are you building this business? What do you specifically hope the end result will be beyond selling products that bring in revenue?"

My client acknowledged the significance of my questions. But they told me, "We don't have time to pause for weeks or months to dive into that right now. We need to go and build this thing."

I understood their point. The clock was ticking, and they wanted to strike while the iron was hot. But I pushed back. "I'm not talking about weeks or months. We have decisions that could be made in one day *if* we take the time to pause now."

The key word there is "if."

Just like my client, it often feels easier to just start running in the direction that *feels* right.

No one is required to pause and get clear on their direction.

But how do we know whether what *feels* right actually *is* right?

How do we know if we're heading in the right direction if we haven't taken time to define our destination?

What if our unvetted feelings lead us toward a place we never wanted to go?

What if, in our rush to move forward, we waste weeks, months, or years investing our TEA in things that turned out to not really matter?

There are really three options here.

- OPTION 1: We can start running, pay no attention to where we're going, and hope we reach a good destination. (Please don't do this.)
- OPTION 2: We can start running, realize we're going in the wrong direction, and have to backtrack and course correct. (Better, but still a waste of precious TEA.)
- OPTION 3: We can invest a little bit of upfront time determining where we're going, plot a course to get there, and then run full speed in that direction.

I'm biased, but at this point in my life and journey, I'm convinced option 3 is *the* option. But option 3 is not about running a million different scenarios and spending months in intense planning trying to decide something. It's creating a brief yet intentional moment in time to stop and answer some key questions about what really matters to us and what Worthy Wins we want all our effort to add up to. (Of course there are scenarios—especially in the business world—where lots and lots of planning is needed, but that's not the situation I'm talking about here.)

Jesus speaks to this when He shares with his followers about the cost of being a disciple. In Luke 14:28–30 (ESV), Jesus says, "For which of you, desiring to build a tower, does not first sit down and count the cost, whether he has enough to complete it? Otherwise, when he has laid a foundation and is not able to finish, all who see it begin mock him, saying, 'This man began to build and was not able to finish.'"[18]

Jesus wasn't saying *not* to build a tower.

He was saying that if you want to build a tower, you can either do the upfront work *or* be made to look foolish.

If building a tower is your goal, fine. But if you don't sit down beforehand to choose what kind of tower you want to build, estimate the costs of building that kind of tower, and decide whether giving up what it costs to build that tower is worth it to you, it's a recipe to ultimately become a *fool*. (Jesus's words, not mine.)

There are several questions that come to mind for me with this metaphor. Why is a tower needed? What problem is the tower going to solve? What is it going to be used for? Who is going to use it? What do you want their experience to be? What resources are available to help you build it? How much time and money is it going to cost to build the kind of tower you want? Can you afford it? What else might need to change to make sure the tower can be built?

Anyone can build a tower.

But these questions will dictate what *type* of tower you build—how high, how wide, what materials, what's on the inside and outside.

Jesus was using the tower as a metaphor to encourage His disciples to think about what it would cost to follow him—everything—and determine whether they were willing to pay that price. He knew that if they didn't decide for themselves that following him was worthy of their TEA, they wouldn't do it. They'd get a little way down the road, and then they'd turn around. Jesus was asking them to do the upfront work of counting the cost *first*.

We all have the opportunity to count the cost in the same way in our own lives. *Everything* has a cost associated with it, and money, time, energy, and attention are not infinite resources.

That's why pausing is so important. It gives us the opportunity to define what winning looks like, determine what it will cost us, and commit to paying that cost so we can go all in toward our Worthy Wins.

Famed IBM CEO Andy Grove said, "There are so many people working so hard and achieving so little."[19]

I don't want that to be my story.

I want the work I do in this life—the way I spend my most valuable resources, my TEA—to be of significance.

I want to spend my time walking down a road that's taking me where I *actually* want to go.

I want my life to matter.

WRITING YOUR OWN OBITUARY

There's one more tricky element to this process. I've shared a lot of examples about how my time at Nike impacted my view of Worthy Wins and how I pursue them in my own life. But there's one major difference between life and work. At work, unless you're self-employed, there's a good chance you're reporting to someone. You have defined expectations, and even though you may have room to determine what Worthy Wins look like within those expectations, you're still accountable for making sure your work is done in a certain way.

In your life, though, you don't have a boss. There's no one officially in charge of what you decide to do with your life. You can't get fired for not doing what you're supposed to do. That means you can either live it to the fullest, pursuing your Worthy Wins and investing your TEA where it matters most, or waste it, wandering aimlessly and going wherever the wind takes you. Both of those are real options, and they're available to every single one of us.

Every business or organization exists to do something. They have a purpose, and that purpose drives the work of every single member of the organization, top to bottom. And so, the question each of us has to answer is:

What do I *specifically* exist to do?

In 2021, the average life expectancy of a US citizen was 76.3 years.[20]

That's 27,868 days.

Which is 668,832 hours.

Which is 40,129,920 minutes.

Those numbers may seem big, but they're not infinite, and anyone who's lived a bit of life knows that years, days, hours, and minutes pass *quickly*. And as I wrote earlier in the chapter, there is this underlying uncertainty we all carry around about how much time we actually will get.

What do you want all of that time to add up to in your life?

I don't believe that we just exist.

I don't think we're here just by chance, a bunch of cogs and gears in some cosmic machine that keeps spinning for no particular reason.

We are people who were each placed on this earth for a reason, each with unique gifts, talents, abilities, circumstances, and challenges. We were meant to spend our lives on something of significance. We just have to determine for ourselves what that "something" is.

Someone once asked legendary businessman and philanthropist Warren Buffet how to best avoid mistakes in business and life. His advice was simple: Write your own obituary and live up to it.[21] Take time to think about what you want to be true at the end of your life, and do everything possible while you're still living to make it true.

Buffet was urging us to consider our legacy.

Because your legacy will be the reverberation from the actions you take over the course of your life.

Put differently, your legacy will be made up of where you invest your TEA.

And the reality is that your legacy will not automatically be positive.

The places where you invest your TEA will determine whether you spend your life winning where it's most worthy to you or at things that are ultimately less important to you. Those investments determine what we're remembered for.

And the truth is this: Every one of us *will* leave a legacy.

The beautiful part is that each of us gets to make choices about what our legacy will be.

While the reality—and the risk—is that our legacy has the potential to be marked by the wrong kinds of wins.

But if we get clear on what it means to win where it's worthy, then we can take ownership of our own legacy by investing our TEA in the right places.

We have the ability to leave behind the kind of legacy we want—one that's defined by our Worthy Wins.

REFLECTION QUESTIONS

These are a few additional questions you can ponder as they relate to your own journey to win where it's worthy.

- Are you clear on the legacy you want to be written about in your obituary?

- When your life is said and done, what are the Worthy Wins you want to have accomplished?

- Who are the specific relationships in your life that you want to invest your limited TEA into?

- What are the specific accomplishments in your life that are worthy of your limited TEA?

PART THREE

HOW TO
WIN

CHAPTER 6

THE BUILDING BLOCKS OF WINNING

WHAT COMES TO mind when you hear the word "fate"?

Each person would probably describe it a bit differently. But generally speaking, most folks would say it's this mysterious, invisible force working behind the scenes to bring about the "right" outcomes.

Some people might even call it destiny.

The place we are bound to end up.

At times in my life—especially the difficult ones—my life has seemed beholden to fate. It's felt like I have no say over the outcome of my days and that whatever is going to happen is going to happen.

But over the last few years, my perspective has begun to evolve. And one thought leader has been particularly helpful to me in that evolution: Donald Miller.

Don is a best-selling author and entrepreneur, and he presents a different perspective about fate in his book *Hero on a Mission*. The very first words he writes in the book after the table of contents are this: "I don't think any of us should trust fate to write the story of our lives. Fate is a terrible writer."[22]

What does he mean?

This is the ignition point for him to let the reader know that they have agency—the idea that we have the ability to act regardless of how bad our circumstances are. We do not have to be bound by the things that happen to us.

We are not stuck.

We have a choice.

Specifically, we have a choice about the story of our lives.

All of us are living a story—whether we like it or not.

Don later tells readers that life *forces* each of us to live a story.

What do we want it to be? And do we want to take control of it? Because if we don't pick up the pen and write it ourselves, we are trusting fate will write it for us. That's basically hoping for the best outcome while leaving everything to chance—which is *not* a recipe for success.

It's like the airport example I referenced in chapter 3. Showing up at an airport and hopping on a random airplane is not an effective way of getting to where you want to go. You have to decide for yourself first where you want to go, and then you have to figure out the best way to get there. If you want to go to the Eiffel Tower, boarding a plane to Australia probably isn't your best route.

That example spells out the two parts of winning where it's worthy: a meaningful story and a strategic plan. In this location example, before ever arriving at the airport you may have decided that your meaningful story is visiting the Eiffel Tower. And once you made that decision, then you must come up with a strategic plan to get there.

Of course, when we're thinking about winning where it's worthy in our lives, the questions get bigger and more significant.

We're no longer just asking what landmark we'd like to visit on our next vacation. We're determining what we want our lives to be about—who we want to be. And, importantly, we're deciding what we will orient our lives around, which determines who we will become in the end.

John Mark Comer says this about stories: "The stories we come to believe give shape to a thousand daily decisions, they give shape to what we do (or don't do) and who we become."[23]

Stories matter.

A meaningful story can spur you on, give you energy and motivation to tackle new challenges, make bold moves, and take risks when you need to. It's a vision of what you want your life to be—something that's personal, intentional, purposeful, and challenging. Believing in your story can drive you to do things you may not have believed you could do. That's a powerful thing.

But a meaningful story can't just be thought.

It *has to* be lived.

So a meaningful story on its own is not enough. We can dream and believe in our meaningful story as much as we want, but if that's all that we do, we'll never get there. A strategic plan is what helps us turn our story into a reality.

We're all busy. We all have a lot of demands on our TEA. Especially those of us with kids. The needs (or shall I say demands?) never stop. Devoting the intentional time it takes to determine a meaningful story and craft a strategic plan is *not* something that happens automatically. Many days, I can't even sit for five minutes of quiet to enjoy my morning cup of tea, let alone have time to think about my story and plan. That means creating intentional time dedicated to this process will be challenging.

But it's worth it.

Having a clear, meaningful story for yourself is *not* the roadmap to win where it's worthy.

It's the starting point—the beginning of your journey toward a specific target, and coupling that meaningful story with a strategic plan creates specific steps to pursue your Worthy Wins. The journey might not always be easy, but having a truly meaningful story and destination helps provide the drive and motivation needed to keep moving forward, even when it's hard.

THE BIG DECLARATION DOMINO

We'll talk more about the nuts and bolts of finding your own meaningful story and strategic plan in the chapters to come. But first, I want to give you a metaphor that's been helpful for me as I've pursued my own Worthy Wins, especially those that seem big or challenging.

Winning where it's worthy
starts with a declaration.

If you make a declaration about what you want to be true of your life—a destination you want to end up at—it initiates a series of events that have the potential to change *everything*.

But aiming for the finish line when you're still standing at the starting line can be daunting. When we set big goals for ourselves—identify wins in our lives that are worthy of our investment but intimidating in their scope—the thought of actually achieving those wins can feel scary.

Impossible, even.

And that initial declaration can be difficult because it creates exposure and risk of failure.

Often, it's easier to avoid going after your meaningful story rather than risk failing.

But holding back because you're scared to fail is *not* a meaningful story.

That's why, instead of viewing this process as one massive undertaking, I like to go back to one simple metaphor: dominoes. When you knock down a long line of dominoes, you don't spend days staring at them, intimidated by their sheer volume, trying to figure out a way to try to do the impossible and flatten them all at once.

You just knock down the first domino.

And if it's set up well, that domino will hit the second domino, which will hit the third domino, and then the fourth, and so on, until the entire line is knocked down. The dominoes ultimately fall one at a time, but it all starts with the initial push.

Winning where it's worthy is just like that. Your declaration is the first domino in your line—the one that gets momentum going. If done right, it will trigger your next domino to fall, and then the next one, and then the next one. But you don't have to knock down all the dominoes at once.

You just focus on the one that's next in line.

I once had a conversation with a man named Paul—better known to his community as Pastor Paul. He was legendary in his town, and he'd seen it all. He'd experienced ups and downs personally, but even more so, he'd walked with others in the good and bad. It was clear he was wise, and at his stage of life, he wanted to find a way to use his wisdom to bless other people.

As we talked, I asked Paul what he wanted to be true about his life a year from now that wasn't currently true. He thought about it, and he landed on an idea that he and his wife had batted around together for a few years now: a podcast dedicated to helping couples stay married.

I *loved* the idea—it was something with real value that could impact people's lives and marriages, and Paul was perfectly positioned to bring it to life. But as we continued chatting, he started getting hung up on all the obstacles in their way.

Their life was *full*—jobs, ministry, kids, a million responsibilities that could keep them from getting this podcast off the ground. Even the thought of launching it within a year felt too daunting.

So, we started talking about the next domino that they could knock down to get closer to launching the podcast. Without even knowing it, Paul had already taken the first step: He had made his declaration. He wanted to pursue this podcast with his wife, with hopes of launching it within a year. But after knocking down that first domino, his focus shifted to the finish line. Rather than staring down the next domino in front of him, he became intimidated by how far he was from his end goal.

I asked Paul, "Have you specifically mapped out what you want to talk about on the podcast?" He told me that they had not. "What if you started with that?" I said. "You could easily map that out in just a few hours."

I saw Paul's eyes widen as the opportunity suddenly became real to him. He didn't need to launch the podcast all in one fell swoop—he just needed to focus on the next domino. That was attainable, and it would move them forward.

I unexpectedly ran into Paul again a few hours after our conversation.

And he was *hyped.*

"I called my wife immediately when I got in the car after we talked," he said. "We're already beginning to plan what we'll talk about on the podcast!"

Paul went from a total standstill to multiple dominoes falling in one day. It started with a declaration, and then it continued moving forward because of a focus on the *next* domino, not the last domino.

In the Bible, it's clear that Jesus had an eternal perspective blended with an awareness of the journey—both in time and challenge—it would take for people to get where they needed to go. He was regularly inviting his followers to focus on the next domino, the next step in front of them. When he called his disciples, he didn't say, "Hey, go be a rabbi right now!" He said, "Follow me." It was an invitation to a daily, step-by-step journey.

But that journey begins with a *first* step in a new direction.

In all compelling stories, there is a moment when everything changes for the hero-to-be. They don't become the hero in an instant. It is a journey.

It takes time and effort to become a hero.

But there has to be an ignition moment to start the journey. Story writers call this an "inciting event," and it is the beginning of the plot for a life that changes for the better. This is the formal term for the proverbial domino moment.

Making a big declaration is an inciting event.

And the beautiful part is that we don't have to wait for it to happen to us.

We are choosing to initiate an inciting event in our lives when we make a declaration about wanting to win where it's worthy.

That's the power of the big declaration domino.

If you haven't begun pursuing your Worthy Wins yet, then the task at hand for you is to ponder what your meaningful story is—what you want to be true about your life in a year, five years, or fifty years that isn't true right now.

Then, make a declaration about it.

Make it official. Put it out into the world.

Share it with a person or two who you trust, who will encourage you on your journey.

Then, start focusing on your next domino. And then the next one. And then the next one.

In the next two chapters, we'll take a closer look at the two parts of winning where it's worthy: a meaningful story and a strategic plan. As we do, and as you begin to explore what it means to win where it's worthy in your own life, don't be intimidated by any part of the process that seems too big, too daunting, too far off to actually attain. Instead, focus on your next step. Figure out what it looks like to knock down your next domino. And eventually, in the end, you'll be looking back from the finish line at a whole line of dominoes that you knocked down, one at a time.

REFLECTION QUESTIONS

These questions can help you ponder the initial steps to get going on winning where it's worthy.

- Is there a declaration you've been waiting to make in your life because it feels too intimidating or scary?

- Who specifically can you share your declaration with that will encourage you on your journey?

- If you have made a declaration, what's the next domino you need to knock down in order to help you move forward?

CHAPTER 7

A MEANINGFUL STORY

AFTER I FINISHED college, I had the amazing opportunity to play basketball for a couple years over in Europe. It was a special season of life that I'm so grateful for, and it was a continuation of my all-consuming identity as a hooper.

I can't count the number of hours I've spent in a gym playing basketball over the years. From the time I was twelve until I turned twenty-seven, basketball was my life. All I wanted to do was become the best player that I could be, so that was the story I adopted and pursued. That meant I crafted specific workout plans to help me improve and evolve my game during those countless hours in the gym. For that season of my life, my story and my actions were in sync.

Yet, even after I "retired" from basketball as my job and started working at Nike, I would frequently head to the gym for a workout and get shots up.

Why?

Because even though basketball wasn't my career anymore, I

was still a hooper, and it felt good to get better. My meaningful story hadn't changed, even though I was in a very different place in life. Basketball was just what I did.

My behavior was on autopilot from the story I had lived for so long.

There's nothing wrong with playing basketball or working to become a better player. I still get in the gym from time to time, even today, because I love the game. But I had a wake-up call when our first son, Jude, was born. Specifically, my free time got crunched. And suddenly, those hours in the gym didn't seem worth it. Why?

Because the story I believed about my life had changed.

Though my identity changed when I "retired" from playing hoops overseas, Jude's birth forced me to acknowledge it for the first time. I was a parent now. Basketball was no longer my primary identity.

And as the story I believed about my life changed, my actions changed along with it.

My friend Justin Kendrick, who is a pastor in Connecticut, puts it this way in his book *Bury Your Ordinary*: "People don't change because they are told to, or even because they want to. We don't change because we should. People usually change their behavior *after* the story of what they believe has been rewritten."[24] (My emphasis in italics.)

In the Bible, Jesus was constantly offering people the chance to rewrite the story they believed about their lives. One of those people was a tax collector named Zaccheus. At that time, being a tax collector carried an extremely negative connotation because they often collected more money from people than they needed to so they could pocket the extra for themselves.

That meant two things for Zaccheus. First, his story and identity were built around being a tax collector, which led to disdain and hatred from the world around him. He was a bad guy in his community. Second, and just as important, even though Zaccheus was gaining wealth from his job, it likely meant he was not very proud of the person he was.

Yet, when Zaccheus heard Jesus was coming to his town one day, he made the effort to go see Him. In Luke 19:1–10, we hear about the story of when they met: "And when Jesus came to the place, he looked up and said to him, 'Zacchaeus, hurry and come down, for I must stay at your house today.' So he hurried and came down and received him joyfully."[25]

The crowd was *indignant*—Jesus was going to stay at the house of a tax collector?

Even Zaccheus himself must have been shocked.

But in that moment, Jesus was offering Zaccheus an opportunity to change the story he believed about himself.

Zaccheus took it.

He invited Jesus into his home. He promised to pay back anyone he had stolen from four times the amount he had taken. He promised to give half of his possessions to the poor. The foundation of his story changed, and with it, his entire life.

Zaccheus's behavior change followed his story, not the other way around.

It was the same as my behavior change with basketball after I embraced the reality of my new story as a father.

When our story changes, everything changes.

Believing in your meaningful story is powerful. And every meaningful story has four pillars: It's personal, intentional, purposeful, and challenging. We'll spend most of the rest of this chapter diving into each of those pillars, explaining why they're important and how to make sure they're true of your meaningful story.

PILLAR 1: PERSONAL—
SPECIFIC AND UNIQUE TO *YOU*

First and foremost, your meaningful story has to be personal.

No two people are exactly alike.

We all have different gifts, different passions, different experiences that inform who we are and what we value. And that's a gift to us all. Living in a world where everyone is exactly the same wouldn't be very fulfilling or very fun.

Austrian psychologist Viktor Frankl, who has an aptly titled book called *Man's Search For Meaning*, has this profound thought: "Life ultimately means taking the responsibility to find the right answer to its problems and to fulfill the tasks which it constantly sets for each individual. These tasks, and therefore the meaning of life, differ from man to man, and from moment to moment. Thus, it is impossible to define the meaning of life in a general way. Questions about the meaning of life can never be answered by sweeping statements."[26]

What does Frankl mean by sweeping statements? Simple: We all have to determine our own meaningful story.

Which means you have to take an active role in finding your own meaningful story.

I can't reveal it to you in this book.

And you can't take someone else's story and make it yours. Acknowledging and leaning into your specific gifting, skills, and circumstances will unlock the door to your meaningful story.

The reason I'm writing this book stems from my own meaningful story. I could have stayed at Nike, kept our family in Oregon, and continued to invest my TEA into the work I'd been doing there. But when I discovered that my personal meaningful story had changed from wanting to lead projects to wanting to invest in people, it shifted everything for me.

Could I have still led giant, complicated marketing projects at Nike? Totally.

But that no longer represented what I *most* wanted to be true about my life. It wasn't the best expression of my gifts, passions, and experiences for where I found myself at the time.

My meaningful story had changed.

And when it became clear that my desire to invest in people wasn't going to be fulfilled in my role at Nike, I had to make a pivot to get to a place where I could have a more direct impact on people.

That's why I do the consulting work that I do now, and it's ultimately why I'm writing this book.

Determining what this looks like for yourself isn't always easy.

A lot of times, it's easier to stick with the status quo and just continue moving in whatever direction we're already moving.

So if that's where you're at—if you're feeling stuck and aren't sure how to determine your own meaningful story—consider these two questions.

First, do you feel that you're living a meaningful life right now?

And second—a question I referenced earlier—what do *you* exist to do?

Or, to put it another way—what's your superpower?

If your answer to the first question is no, then considering your answer to the second question would be a great place to start. What are your gifts, the unique talents that God has given you to bring to the world? What are your passions, the things that fire you up, that drive you to do your best work, that are constantly coming up in your mind and in your conversations? What have you experienced that might equip you to bring your gifts and passions together in a meaningful way?

There's no wrong answer to any of these questions—as long as you answer in a way that's honest and authentic to *you*.

Winning where it's worthy is *not* about quitting your job. (Even though I did.)

In *Halftime,* famed cable TV pioneer and philanthropist Bob Buford says this about reconsidering your aim and what it may mean, "That might involve a completely new career or holding on to your present position. Usually, it is something between the two."[27]

So, it's about stopping to get clear about what you're going to aim at. What are you going to direct your life toward?

What story is meaningful enough that it's worth investing all of your TEA?

Maybe that *does* mean you'll end up quitting your job. But maybe it means something completely different. There's no obligation in any of this.

Worthy Wins are about opportunity, not obligation.

Opportunity to define success.

Opportunity to use your specific superpowers (because you *absolutely* have unique, specific superpowers).

Opportunity to invest your TEA where it matters most.

Opportunity to identify your meaningful story and live into it.

The first step is simply to make space to think about it. Create time now to explore a meaningful story that's personal to *you*. Ask yourself what *you* want to be true at the end of your life so *you* can live with the end in mind.

If you wonder why I keep using *you* in italics, it's because this is all about *you*.

Not me.

Not someone else.

Not your company.

You.

It's personal to *you.*

Maybe you're in a position where a career change or another big shift is what you want, but your circumstances and responsibilities won't allow it right now. That's okay! Ask yourself what you can do to find meaning in your current situation? How can you live within your present reality to make your life as meaningful as possible?

These aren't always easy questions to answer. But if you've determined what the personal elements of your meaningful story look like, you're at least giving yourself the opportunity to explore them. You're awakening a new awareness within yourself of what would make your life truly meaningful. And that's a critical foundation to build from.

PILLAR 2: INTENTIONAL— COMMITMENT TO A *SPECIFIC* DIRECTION

In chapter 6, I mentioned the very first words in Donald Miller's book *Hero on a Mission.* Don was imploring us not to let fate write our story because the people we view as heroes—whether in real life or in just about every movie, book, or play—have not allowed fate to determine their story.

Later in the book, Don talks about the need to get *specific*: "A storyteller must define an exact thing the hero wants. They want to win the karate tournament. They want to save their father's company. They want to marry their sweetheart. Once the hero defines what they want, the story begins."[28]

We can see the journey play out in almost every movie, book, play, or other story we've ever been moved by. The basic structure is the same: The hero has something they are trying to achieve (a clear, *specific* target), they encounter obstacles in their path, they overcome the obstacles, and ultimately they succeed in their quest. But the journey wouldn't happen without the starting point Don was talking about: the hero's intentional decision to pursue something *specific* that matters to them.

Meaningful stories don't just happen. They have to be chosen.

We have to do more than figure out what story would be meaningful to us—we have to make an intentional commitment. This means aiming our lives in a *specific* direction, willing to let other things fall by the wayside in order to stay committed to the story we're pursuing.

In the Bible, the apostle Paul is an interesting example of this in action. Though he wrote big chunks of the New Testament and is viewed now as a pioneer of the gospel and mission work, Paul was originally headed in a completely different direction. He even had a different name: Saul.

And Saul was *not* a pioneer of the gospel.

He actually sought to persecute and punish followers of Jesus. That was his identity, the story that guided his life. And you have to give him credit—he was definitely committed to it.

But then, he encountered Jesus on the road to Damascus, and everything changed. Romans 9:3–5 says, "Now as he went on his way, he approached Damascus, and suddenly a light from heaven shone around him. And falling to the ground, he heard a voice saying to him, 'Saul, Saul, why are you persecuting me?' And he said, 'Who are you, Lord?' And he said, 'I am Jesus, whom you are persecuting.'"[29]

During this interaction with Jesus, Saul lost his sight. His vision was gone, both literally and metaphorically. His eyes could no longer see, and at the same time, the vision he'd had for his life before had disappeared. Everything he had been living for vanished in a moment.

Saul did what Jesus told him to do next, going into Damascus (with help from his travel companions) and meeting with a man named Ananias. He listened to what Ananias told him, had his sight restored, and was baptized.

After this, the direction of Saul's life dramatically shifted. His name changed from Saul to Paul. He immediately began preaching about Jesus (to the amazement of people who recognized him from his former life). He quickly found himself in harm's way, a target of the same persecution he used to direct at followers of Jesus. After spending several days preaching in Damascus, he even had to flee for his life. His meaningful story had shifted.

He had made an intentional choice and was fully committed to his new, *specific* direction.

Meaningful stories require intention.

Paul wouldn't have gone on to lead so many people to know Jesus in the early days of the church if he hadn't intentionally committed to the direction Jesus had led him in. I wouldn't be writing this book if I hadn't made an intentional choice to dedicate my life to pouring into other people.

And it's the same for all of us. If we want to bring our meaningful stories to life—if we want them to be more than just stories—we have to intentionally commit to them.

PILLAR 3: PURPOSEFUL— SEEKING A GREATER GOOD

What does it mean to seek a greater good?

For me, the answer goes back to a question I've asked many times already in this book: What do I want to be true about my life when it's over? When all is said and done, what would I want to celebrate (or be celebrated) on my deathbed? What do I want to be said about me at my funeral?

Any of us could devote our lives to individual accolades. There's so much to be accomplished.

But will that lead to a life that's truly meaningful?

How will it feel at the end of our lives if the only things we've accomplished are self-focused, self-oriented, self-promoting?

For me, not great.

I want the stories told at my funeral to be about how I loved and cared about other people.

In *The Secret Society of Success*, my friend Tim Schurrer offers a succinct reminder about the focal point of a meaningful story. He writes, "When you make the people around you better, that's when you truly win."[30]

I hope people will remember me that way: for how I gave of my own life to make others' lives better.

Imagining stories being told about my selfishness, my stinginess, my unrelenting drive to get to the top at all costs just sounds depressing.

And if that were the case, there might not be anyone there to tell those stories anyway.

Prior to his encounter with Jesus, Saul didn't have a meaningful story. Can you imagine reaching the end of your life and the only thing you had to celebrate was how much success you had persecuting others?

Thankfully, that wasn't the end of his story. When Saul became Paul, he went from persecuting Christ-followers to seeking a greater good for the world. He dedicated his life to helping people experience the transformative power of Jesus. In his own words, he lived his life so that people's "love may abound more and more, with knowledge and all discernment, so that you may approve what is excellent, and so be pure and blameless for the day of Christ, filled with the fruit of righteousness that comes through Jesus Christ, to the glory and praise of God."[31]

That's the kind of greater good that deserves to be celebrated at the end of someone's life. And I believe that for any story to be meaningful, the greater good has to be a part of it. Living a self-focused story may feel gratifying at the moment and make you look successful to the world.

But outward success does not equal lasting meaning.

Your "greater good" might not be the same as Paul's. (Let's be honest—not many of us are meeting Jesus, losing and then regaining our eyesight, preaching the gospel, and then getting lowered by a basket to escape a city without losing our lives.) Maybe your greater purpose is raising your kids well, or taking care of an aging family member, or doing work that will encourage or help other people.

Since meaningful stories are personal, a greater purpose will look different for each of us.

But one thing is true for all of us: If we want to live a story that's truly meaningful, the greater good has to be a part of it. That means looking beyond ourselves and seeking to serve others.

PILLAR 4: CHALLENGING—
DIFFICULT OR UNCERTAIN TO ACHIEVE

Robert McKee is a famous story-writing consultant. Maybe *the* most famous teacher of story writing ever. He has taught more than a hundred thousand people all over the world about how to write great stories—including some of the most celebrated writers in the world—sixty of his students have won Academy Awards, and two hundred have won Emmys, among many other writing awards.

In short, he knows how to help people write meaningful stories.

And this is what he says about the best stories. "Nothing moves forward in a story except through conflict."[32]

That means we *need* conflict, challenge, and difficulty to help write a great story for our lives.

But that doesn't mean it's enjoyable in the midst of that.

I once had a boss who liked to say, "If anybody could do this, we'd be out of a job."

He would typically say it in very tense and stressful moments when things looked *bleak* and we were frustrated by the challenges in front of us. In those moments, his words felt like someone running their fingernails down a chalkboard.

The last thing I wanted to hear when things were hard was that it was supposed to be hard.

But deep down, if I was honest with myself, I knew he was right.

Challenging circumstances make success that much more valuable.

And if something is easy to achieve, it ultimately doesn't end up being very fulfilling.

I'm guessing you might intuitively realize the truth behind this. At a deep level, we can sense that the most meaningful things in life don't come easily. The word "worthwhile" is literally a shortened version of the phrase "worth your while" or worth your time. If something is worthwhile—if it's *worthy*—you're going to have to invest time and elbow grease in it. By definition, Worthy Wins are going to demand something from you.

At times—or basically all the time in the midst of difficulty—it feels like life would be better if we didn't have to deal with those hard things. Bearing our way through challenges can feel like suffering—or, in some cases, is literal suffering. Our bodies and minds don't like to suffer. But getting rid of that pain is not realistic.

In *Build the Life You Want*, Harvard professor Arthur C. Brooks and global icon Oprah Winfrey talk about the benefits of difficult circumstances. But they clarify this is more about inevitability rather than wanting to suffer. "Perhaps you are wondering if we are suggesting that you look for suffering. There's no need; suffering *will* find you—and everyone else."[33] (My emphasis in italics.)

They also are abundantly clear about the opportunity we have amidst this reality: "The common strategy of trying to eliminate suffering from life to get happier is futile and mistaken; we must instead look for the why of life to make pain an opportunity for growth."[34]

Since challenges are inevitable and meaningful stories are personal, the difficulties are not going to look the same for everyone.

It can be challenging to build a rocket, to be a teacher, or to advocate for your special needs child. It can and will mean different things to different people.

But the constant is this: Challenge adds meaning.

The desire to accomplish something difficult or uncertain is a good thing. It can keep you interested in your meaningful story and motivate you to put in the work. It can engage you more deeply in your pursuit of Worthy Wins. It can give you a reason to get up in the morning, dig deeper, work to overcome obstacles. Without something challenging to go after, it's easy to gravitate toward the status quo and just follow the flow of life.

Chances are, if your meaningful story meets the first three pillars—personal, intentional, and purposeful—it's already a challenging story. If you've created a story that represents what you want to be true of your life when it's over, it's probably not going to be a cakewalk.

If dreams were easy to achieve, we wouldn't call them dreams.

They'd just be lines on a checklist, mundane everyday tasks that anyone could accomplish.

For a story to be meaningful, it *has to* require hard work.

There's a flip side to that, though. If your meaningful story is challenging, that means there are going to be times when it might feel easier to just give up. There might be moments when you fail or when continuing on might feel impossible.

Or when it hurts so much that you can't see how it could possibly lead to anything good.

Or when the skies of life are so dark that you can't see them ever clearing.

And in those moments, I'd remind you what my boss reminded me in difficult moments, but in a more empathetic way: The challenges are not fun, but you can get through them, and they will make your story more meaningful.

The end result will be worth it.

Living a meaningful story is a Worthy Win.

In those challenging moments, the other three pillars of your meaningful story come in. Yes, your meaningful story is challenging, but it's also personal, uniquely suited to your gifts, passions, and experience. It's intentional, something you chose from the beginning and committed to, even though you knew it wouldn't be easy. And it's purposeful, dedicated to a greater purpose that you believe in.

Those other three pillars work together to help you push through moments of challenge—to stay committed to your meaningful story, even though it isn't easy.

MEANING IN EVERYTHING

Defining your meaningful story is an incredibly powerful step, and when combined with a strategic plan (which we'll talk about in the next chapter), it can help carry you to Worthy Wins in your life. But we shouldn't end our conversation without acknowledging a hard truth: We don't always have control over what happens in our story.

My mom died when I was eleven. It was the moment my innocence was shattered. I was a child dealing with heartache and sadness that I didn't know how to process.

I was confused, trying to grasp why and how something like that could happen.

I knew my life was never going to be the same.

Over time, I realized that I had no choice but to accept reality: People die, and many times, it will feel unfair. I could choose to disconnect, to believe that because hard things happen, life must not matter—that we're all just here randomly and nothing has any meaning.

Or I could choose to believe that all of life has meaning, even the hard parts.

I started this chapter talking about Dr. Viktor Frankl, and it's fitting to wrap up with more of his story. He was more than just an Austrian psychiatrist—he was a Holocaust survivor. He spent a great deal of time in a concentration camp in Auschwitz, suffering and figuring out how to stay alive. If anyone could understand what it means to search for meaning in suffering, it would be him.

Frankl wrote, "If there is a meaning in life at all, then there must be a meaning in suffering. Suffering is an ineradicable part of life, even as fate and death. Without suffering and death, human life cannot be complete."[35]

The veil that was lifted as I went through the grieving process for my mom showed me a lifelong, indisputable truth that we also see from Frankl's experience and writing:

I have a choice in how I respond to hardship.

My mom's death woke me up to the reality of how short life can be.

And my dad's death reminded me of that painful reality so many years later.

But both of those experiences showed me that for however long I have, I want to dedicate my life to things that matter.

As I've reflected on those realities and my own meaningful story, there is another truth that I keep coming back to:

I control the inputs, but I don't always control the outputs.

I can invest everything I have into something, but I'm not in total control. There's no guarantee that my business will succeed, that the time I invest in people will pay off, or that the cross-country move we made will work out the way we'd imagined.

But the truth is, a meaningful story isn't about the outputs.

When you define your meaningful story, you're not just saying, "This is what I want to do."

You're saying, "This is who I want to be."

You're declaring that your decisions are going to be driven by what you want to be most true of your life—the very core of who you are.

We can find meaning in hard things because, like Frankl said, if any of life has meaning, then suffering must have meaning, too. And we can continue to pursue our meaningful story even in the midst of challenge, pain, and disappointment.

Our circumstances may change what our lives look like. But they don't have to change who we are.

YOUR STORY, ALREADY IN PROGRESS

Here's an undeniable reality: Everyone is writing a story. At the end of your life, you will have a story to look back on.

It's not optional.

What *is* optional is the kind of story you want to write.

Your story is already in progress. But taking time to define what you want your meaningful story to look like—something that's personal, intentional, purposeful, and challenging—will help you make it the story you want to tell. And when combined with a strategic plan, that will help you win where it's worthy. Let's build the plan.

REFLECTION QUESTIONS

These questions can help you reflect on the current state of your story and how to begin to make it more meaningful.

- Have you gotten clear about what *you* specifically exist to do?

- What story do you believe about your life right now? Is it the story you want your life to tell?

- What are one or two ways you can intentionally lean into your personal story?

- What is the greater good that you can purposefully seek out in your story?

- What does it look like to find meaning in challenges you've experienced in your life?

CHAPTER 8

A STRATEGIC PLAN

THE SUMMER AFTER I finished grad school, there was an inevitable question brewing with every person I talked to.

Everyone was well-intentioned.

And it was a totally reasonable question.

But that didn't mean I wanted to answer it.

What was that inevitable question?

"So, what's your plan now?"

Every time it came up, I felt a surge of anxiety pulse through my body.

I was in my early twenties, and—between my undergrad and graduate studies—I'd spent the last six years as a relatively successful student athlete. That had been my identity, my meaningful story, my solitary focus.

So why was I pulsing with anxiety when this question came up?

Because I did *not* have a plan.

I felt completely exposed by the question. I hadn't decided what I wanted to do with my life now that being a student athlete was coming to a close.

There were some unique circumstances at play. I was scheduled to have jaw surgery a few months after graduation, so I didn't have an immediate job lined up. Instead, I had decided I was going to spend the summer working at a homeless shelter, with the hope of writing a book about my experience. Far from the traditional journey after graduating with an MBA. I was excited and doing my best to embrace it, but there was no long-term direction or plan.

Despite my lack of direction, that summer was extremely impactful for me. It was the first time in my young adult life that I wasn't accomplishing things that were significant in the eyes of the world. In the end, I realized that I didn't want to hitch my personal worth to my accomplishments.

And more importantly, it unlocked a truth that I hold onto today:

Who I am is *not* what I do.

Let me say it again as a reminder to myself and to you: Who I am is not what I do.

So, there was plenty of good that came from my summer after grad school. I'm thankful that God can and does use our imperfect choices, decisions, and circumstances to bring about good.

But eventually, it became obvious to me that I was lacking direction—that I hadn't taken the time to step back and look for a bigger vision for my life. I had just been going with the flow, being 'successful' as a student athlete, with no idea what I wanted the meaningful story of my life to be in the long run.

Without that, it was almost impossible for me to decide what to do next with my life. Working at the homeless shelter was a good stopgap, but it wasn't the endgame for me. And thankfully, one of the additional positives that came out of it for me was the learning experience about the importance of a strategic plan. It wasn't the last time I was going to face an inflection point in my life.

Fast-forward fifteen years to October 2022, and I was getting asked the *exact* same question I heard after finishing my MBA. Every person I talked to wanted to know what I was going to do after Nike. But there was one major difference this time: As I left Nike, I had a clear picture of what I wanted to be true of my life when it was over.

And that one thing changed everything.

I would define my decade at Nike as a success for me personally. There was much to be proud of, and I was walking away whole—as a whole individual who was still following Jesus, with an intact marriage and family to show for it—along with the success from the work itself. I had won where it was worthy.

That meant I was walking *away* from success.

But this time, I was clear about where I was headed.

I no longer had the prestige and aura of saying I worked at Nike. But I had something else—something I didn't have when I finished my MBA: I was walking toward my meaningful story. I wasn't just looking for a stopgap solution.

The trepidation I felt every time that question came up after my graduation was nowhere to be found. Don't let me fool you— leaving Nike wasn't easy. I was scared. But I was also very clear about what mattered most to me. And that clarity allowed me to move forward with confidence toward the meaningful story I wanted to pursue.

A clear story creates clear steps.

Defining the meaningful story I wanted to live out in my life helped me be prepared when it was time to step into that new journey. And it formed a bridge to the strategic plan that would help get me there.

That's the second half of winning where it's worthy: a strategic plan. Once we've defined our meaningful story, the target is clear. But we still need to answer the question: How do we actually get to the wins we most want to achieve?

That's the purpose of a strategic plan. It gives us the specific steps we need to take to bring our meaningful story to life.

To win where it's *worthy*.

And from my experience both at Nike and in my personal life, I've found that the most effective strategic plans have four steps: objective, strategy, execution, and reflection. We'll spend the rest of this chapter exploring each of them, hopefully leaving you with a clear picture of how to use this method to bring your own meaningful story to life.

OBJECTIVE

When I worked at Nike, I spent *a lot* of time building strategic plans. Marketing plans, athlete plans, platform plans.

Plans on plans on plans.

And the best plans, the ones that went on to bring the most success, always had one thing in common: a clear objective.

Without that clarity, we couldn't align around what success looked like, which would make it impossible to develop a coherent strategy. That's why our approach to Mamba Week had been so important. We took the time up front to clearly and explicitly define what winning looked like. A clear objective gave us something to shoot for collectively, and it clarified our target as we developed a strategy.

If our objective isn't clear, then the decisions on where to focus our TEA won't be clear either.

The good news is that if you've taken time to define your meaningful story, your objective should flow pretty naturally from that. Once you've decided what you want to be true of your life, you can determine what specific objective you need to pursue.

Let me give you a nonwork example—one where no one was paying me to develop a strategy. One of the most important Worthy Wins in my life is being connected with my wife, Erin. It's a huge part of my own meaningful story. With young kids, work, and all the busyness of life, it's easy for each of us to go into survival mode just to get through each day.

There are a lot of things in our lives that naturally foster *disconnection.*

When we moved from Oregon to Florida, COVID was beginning to lighten up, and we were able to start having a weekly date night. It was awesome to get out and be together, especially coming from peak COVID time in Oregon when we were inside with our kids all day, every day. Having the chance to go on a date and just talk to each other—uninterrupted—was incredible.

But the busyness of life found a way to catch up with us, even on these once-a-week date nights. We quickly found that our "dates" were turning into our "dumps": brain dumps, calendar dumps, kid dumps.

All the things we didn't have a spare moment to discuss during the week were coming up on our dates instead. We were still getting time together, but the time was no longer focused on connecting as a couple.

One day, Erin said out loud what both of us were feeling: She wasn't really enjoying our dates. They had begun to feel just like another part of our busy lives, and they were not helping us stay connected in the way they once were.

Erin and I both agreed that staying connected to each other was a critical part of our meaningful story. So, now we had a new objective: creating space in our lives to allow that connection. We were ready to find a strategy to help us get there.

STRATEGY

Your objective is the "what." But to achieve it, you need to figure out your "how." You need a strategy.

Strategies are the things you do broadly to help you achieve your aim. They're the consistent actions you can take to help you get the outcome you want. They make your idea into something practical, something you can put into action.

Another term I like to use when I think about strategy is *active intentions*. Defining your meaningful story helps you hone in on what your intentions are. But the next step is to develop consistent actions that will lead to those intentions becoming reality. When I combine intentions with consistent actions, I create *active* intentions.

Imagine telling the most important people in your life that you love them and want to spend more time with them and then doing nothing about it.

Would your words matter to those people?

Would the intention you expressed to invest more time in your relationship have gotten you anywhere?

No.

You can have the greatest intentions in the world, but if you don't make them into active intentions, they won't get you anywhere.

Here's a simple question to ask yourself when you're developing a strategy: What actions can I take consistently to turn my intentions into *active* intentions? This is one of the most important steps toward achieving your Worthy Wins. It's the bridge between your objective and execution, where you actually get to put your plan into action.

When Erin and I agreed that our objective was to create space in our lives to stay connected as a couple, we knew we needed a strategy to get there. We were blessed to have Erin's parents nearby, and her mom's willingness to watch our kids one night each week so we could have a date night was an *incredible* gift. But we couldn't ask for more date nights, as nice as that would be. So, we needed to find a way to create more intentional time together without having more nights out of the house.

As parents of three young kids, we knew we needed to get more strategic about our time together.

Quality time doesn't just happen. It has to be intentionally created.

So, we needed a strategy to ensure that time happened and that, when it did, it was actually helping us be more connected.

Because this was about keeping our relationship strong, consistency was crucial.

In *The Good Life: Lessons from the World's Longest Scientific Study of Happiness*, the authors reveal this truth about intimate relationships: "Even the best relationships are susceptible to decay. Just as trees need water, intimate relationships are living things, and as the seasons of life pass they can't be left to fend for themselves. They need attention, and nourishment."[36]

So, in addition to our weekly date night, we decided to add two intentional and consistent connection points to our week to provide that nourishment. The first was a weekly planning meeting, which we could use as an opportunity to debrief on all the life stuff we had previously been using our date nights to talk about. Schedules, plans, tasks, responsibilities—this would be our intentional opportunity to get aligned on everything, which we hoped would allow us freedom to spend our date nights in the way we wanted to as well.

We dubbed our second connection point "Wine Wednesday." This, we decided, would be the night of the week we would block off just for *us*. Weeknights can be crazy with kid commitments, friend commitments, and school commitments, but we decided we'd commit to Wednesday nights as a sacred time for us to connect after our kids go to bed.

Wine Wednesday isn't formal.

And most Wednesdays, we don't even drink wine.

But we do create consistent, intentional space to connect on Wednesday nights. It could be talking, watching a movie or show together, even just sitting together in silence—anything we feel we need at that time. And the crucial point for us is that we know, *every* Wednesday, we will get to connect because we have protected the time in advance.

We had our strategy. But a strategy, no matter how well thought-out, doesn't mean anything unless you actually put it into action.

EXECUTION

When I worked at Nike, there were a few different structures put in place to support big initiatives. These structures didn't take away from the work that had to be done by individuals, but they were there to make sure that the work kept moving forward on track.

Every team or organization within Nike had their own set of dates and gates that directed their schedules and priorities. In the world of marketing—my world—there were specific checkpoints for every season. We started with business alignment and eventually moved into creative brief, marketing review 1, marketing review 2, and then the final marketing review, which was meant to be the end of the road where we'd get all our work approved and ready to go to market.

Could we have executed marketing work without the structures in place?

Sure.

Would both the work process and the end result have been chaotic?

Yes, 100 percent.

We needed to build and use systems and structures to help us execute our strategy.

There are more productivity systems and plans out there than you could ever experiment with in one lifetime. What kind of system you use isn't the point—it can look different based on your needs and preferences. But regardless of *which* system we use, I believe it's important that we all have *a* system that helps us execute with excellence.

The idea of a detailed project management system can seem pretty daunting, especially when you remove it from a work context and think about it in your personal life. But there can be a *simple* starting point for making a change, and it's born out of the idea that consistency is the key to success.

It starts by answering this simple question, one that you probably already know the answer to if you've developed a strategy: What are the actions I need to take with *consistency* that will lead me toward my intentional desires?

Consistency is the key to executing with excellence and getting Worthy Wins.

It's what truly puts your active intentions into action.

That's what the structures and systems at Nike were about—creating consistency in the way we worked to lead us toward intentional outcomes. But you don't have to start by being consistent at a thousand things or some big process like Nike. You can start with one area related to one of your Worthy Wins. Figure out a system that works for you—something sustainable and focused on consistency. And then, as you find success in that one area, start to apply your system to other areas as well.

For Erin and me, executing with consistency simply looked like blocking out time on our calendar to make room for our newly scheduled connection points. We've found that over time, the way we use the time we've blocked off can evolve—for example, our weekly planning meeting often branches beyond schedules and to-do lists to include deeper conversations around things that have been joyful or difficult over the past week or how we are each feeling about our connection. But consistency is what makes our strategy work.

Our "system" isn't monumental. It's not crazy or even particularly ambitious. But it is simple and consistent.

As a result of these choices, we now have three intentional connection times each week rather than just one, and it's been a game changer for our relationship.

Three times the intentional time that we had before.

From fifty-two intentional times connecting in a year to one hundred fifty-six.

And we've seen over time how this little system has had a huge impact on drawing us together—for us to be connected and win where it's worthy, together.

Extrapolate out ten years, and that gap is more than a thousand intentional connection points. If our aim is to be connected, this is a *really* significant difference.

Consistency in execution is what's needed in order to get Worthy Wins. If we can identify the actions we need to get us to our Worthy Wins—even if those actions are simple—and then put them in place with consistency, then we will execute with excellence.

REFLECTION

Even when we've made it through the first three phases of our strategic plan—objective, strategy, and execution—it can be easy for us to become complacent, succumb to the busyness of life, and fall into a new status quo. That's why the fourth step in the process is so crucial. If we're going to continue pursuing Worthy Wins in our lives—not just once, but for a lifetime—we have to take time to reflect.

Famous American philosopher John Dewey urged the importance of creating time to look back on our experiences, "We do not learn from experience.... We learn from reflecting on experience."[37]

A Harvard Business School study found that reflection improves performance and noted that it even leads to a greater perceived ability to reach a goal.[38] When we take time to reflect, we increase both our competence and confidence in our ability to achieve more of our Worthy Wins.

This does not have to be complicated.

Reflecting, at its core, is just pausing to ask ourselves how things are going.

I use a simple framework to help me pause and reflect. I call it the WLOPs Framework—*wins, losses, and opportunities* for improvement. Whenever I reflect on an area of my life, those are the categories I use. I ask myself a few simple questions:

- What were my wins? (What should I keep doing?)
- What were my losses? (What should I stop doing?)
- Where do I have opportunities to improve? (What new things should I start doing? What things should I try doing differently?)

One of the most pivotal changes Erin and I have made is an annual reflection exercise we've begun doing, both individually and as a couple. We block off a few hours to take inventory of different areas of our lives and go through the questions I listed above. In doing so, I go through the WLOPs Framework as it relates to my own health (spiritually, physically, and emotionally), Erin, our family, my friends, and my work.

Then Erin and I talk about our individual reflections, and we reflect together on how we feel the last year went in our marriage and with our family.

This has been a game changer for our relationship—and our lives.

Because we've taken the time to reflect, it's created conversations that celebrate the successes of the previous year, and it's created a venue for us to discuss what needs to be added, changed, or removed to help us win where it's worthy.

In short, these reflections have made us better as individuals, as a couple, and as parents.

And then once we've reflected, the process begins again for the year ahead.

The beautiful thing about reflection is that while it's the last step of the process, it also leads back to the start of a new process.

The end is the beginning.

Once you finish your reflection, you go back to the start—clearly defining the objectives and then creating a strategy to move toward the objective along with the changes you've identified from the reflection work.

Check in on your meaningful story—has it changed? Do you need to adjust based on things that may have shifted in your life or in your heart? Then, based on what you learned in your time of reflection, go back through your objectives, strategy, and execution, making tweaks where you need to.

None of this is a one-time process.

Winning where it's worthy is a daily journey.

If you want to look back at the end of your life and be happy with the journey you've taken, it's going to take a lifetime of commitment. But if you combine the two concepts we've discussed over the last two chapters—a meaningful story and a strategic plan—you have everything you need to win where it's worthy.

REFLECTION QUESTIONS

- Has your meaningful story created clarity about what Worthy Wins you want to pursue?

- Have you created a strategy that will help you succeed in those areas?

- Similar to Erin's and my story about blocking time on our calendars for our intentional touchpoints, how and where can you create blocked-off time to consistently pursue your Worthy Wins?

- When will you specifically make time to reflect on your pursuit of your Worthy Wins and whether or not your strategic plan is working? How will you know if your plan is working? How will you know if it is *not*?

CHAPTER 9

TENSIONS AND PITFALLS

DOES THIS ALL sound too good to be true?

Too much rah-rah and smell the roses for you?

Are you saying, "Hey John, I love your optimism, but life happens, and it's *hard*."

Great. Me too. I'm with you.

And as much as we might wish we did, we don't have complete control over our own lives. I acknowledged this earlier: We can do all the planning and strategizing and executing and reflecting that we want to, but life can throw us curve balls.

We control the inputs, not the outputs.

Sometimes when life throws one of those curveballs, we're going to swing and miss. That's just how it is. But other times, if we're aware that it's coming, we can adjust for the curveball and still connect.

I mentioned my friend Tim Schurrer in chapter 7. In *The Secret Society of Success*, he also writes this, "There are tensions all around us, and the biggest mistake we can make is to believe we can solve them."[39]

Tim elaborates, "To be at our best, we've got to live in the tension between the push and pull, the inhales and exhales of life."[40]

So, are we stuck with tension?

In short, yes.

And there are certain tensions and pitfalls that are common obstacles in pursuing Worthy Wins. But if we're aware of them, we can plan intentionally so they don't derail us completely. In this chapter, we're going to walk through five potential areas that can trip us up—what they are, how to recognize them, and what we can do to move past them.

BALANCE AND COUNTERBALANCE

Balance.

That elusive thing so many of us are chasing—and struggling to catch hold of.

In his book, *The Mamba Mentality: How I Play*, Kobe had a profound word for us all: "You can't achieve greatness by walking a straight line."[41]

Did he mean balance was incompatible with greatness? Possibly, but I think he actually meant that expecting balance and greatness at the same time wasn't possible.

This makes me think of an eye-opening conversation I had over breakfast with a pastor named Daniel Grothe. I was impressed with the work he was doing at a large church, and I asked him how he balanced his work with being present to his family. His answer surprised me.

"Balance is a myth."

Whoa.

It felt like a mic drop, but I wanted him to tell me more.

After letting his words sink in for a moment, he explained that in order to accomplish meaningful things, there would be times when we would have to move *out* of balance. There will always be a significant cost—time, money, opportunity, or all of the above—and sometimes staying balanced while paying that cost won't be possible.

Instead, Daniel said, he focuses on *counterbalance* when it comes to being connected to his family. He shared with me how communication, planning, and intentional "counter-investments" formed the critical bedrock for his family. There were busy seasons, but he made it a point to counterinvest TEA in his family so that when those more demanding seasons came, he would have put reserves in place. He counterbalanced seasons of high investment at work with highly intentional investment into his family.

Daniel went on to use the example of a helicopter. "You'll notice that every helicopter has two rotors, not just one," he said. "Why? Because helicopters require a counterbalance to fly. Their flight pattern would be out of control if they only had one rotor, creating lift and force. The second rotor comes into play to create counterbalance that allows for safe, controlled flying."

This idea hit me hard because I want to win—at work *and* with the people I love.

You know this by now if you're still reading this book.

But I had been wrestling with whether or not balance was actually possible, especially in the midst of crazy seasons on the work front.

And it turns out, "balance" per se is not actually possible.

But counterbalance is.

Daniel's explanation of the concept of counterbalance left me with one major takeaway: I needed more than one rotor.

This new mindset was a game changer for me. One rotor of my life was the work I had to get done, but the counterbalancing rotor was an intentional investment in my family. If I knew I was entering a heavy week of work where it might be hard for me to make it home for dinner, I'd work to prepare beforehand. I'd mark off a few nights on my calendar where I'd prioritize making it home for dinner no matter what, and a few days before my crazy stretch of work started, I'd take time off of work to be present and spend extra time with Erin and the boys.

I recently had an important meeting scheduled with a consulting client on a day when Jude, my oldest son, didn't have school. Our babysitter was originally supposed to come over and watch him, but she had to cancel.

True balance was pretty much impossible to achieve in that moment. I needed to be in this meeting, but I also wanted to be able to spend time with Jude when he was home from school and demonstrate to him that he was important to me.

This was a counterbalance opportunity. It was physically impossible for me to go to my meeting *and* spend the whole day with Jude, so I explained to him that I needed to take this call, but that, afterward, we'd spend some time having fun together. He agreed to let me take my call in "peace" (and then proceeded to come in three times during the meeting to ask when I'd be done—thankfully, my client was gracious!).

After the meeting was over, Jude presented me with his plan for what he wanted to do together, and we spent the rest of the day making it happen. It's a small example, but by communicating with Jude up front and making an intentional investment with him when I could, I was able to make my son feel valued while still prioritizing work. This was a real-life counterbalance.

The most important investments in life—professional or personal—are going to cost you. Pursuing your most meaningful Worthy Wins can have a great impact, but there will be times when they will throw your life out of balance. Employing counterbalance can help make sure other important areas of your life don't get neglected.

EMBRACING THE GRAY AREAS

Have you ever had a moment when you felt torn between two important things and didn't know what to do?

I've spent the past several years reading through the entire New Testament over the course of the year, and as a result, I've started picking up on themes. One theme that I can't seem to ignore is that Jesus *lived* in the gray areas.

He challenged religious leaders on their definition of the Sabbath.

He encouraged people to love their enemies.

He invested in people who were cast out by society.

Among many other things that bridged between the black-and-white dichotomies of that time.

He was intentional with his time and clear on his mission, but he was always interruptible by people who needed him.

And when leaders tried to challenge him by forcing him to choose one of two paths, He chose a third path instead.

Jesus consistently embraced the gray areas and encouraged others to do the same.

I recently went on a trip to Orlando with my family shortly after New Year's, right at the tail end of our kids' Christmas break from school. It was the first time when the reality—and tradeoffs—of owning my own business became obvious.

I was able to travel when I wanted, which was great. But an important realization took place on this trip: I didn't get paid time off anymore, and there weren't other people keeping my business running for me while I was gone.

Obvious, *right*?

But I had been a corporate employee for so long I was just used to being able to be fully off when I was on PTO.

This was a family trip, and I didn't want to spend my time working. But completely pressing pause on my business really wasn't an option for me during this particular time. So, I communicated that with my family, and then I got up super early one morning of the trip to work for a few hours. I never would have had to do that on the family vacations we took during my time at Nike.

But my new reality brought with it new gray areas.

My choice to leave the corporate world and work as a consultant so I could prioritize my family more highly came with tradeoffs that didn't always feel great at the time.

Here's my encouragement to you: Embrace the complexity that comes with pursuing your Worthy Wins. You're going to run into questions at times that don't have easy answers. I didn't love having to work while on vacation with my family. But I was doing it in support of the bigger-picture meaningful story that I was working to align my life with. I wanted to do work that allowed me to pour into other people and that enabled me to spend more time with my family overall. It was a tradeoff to have to pull out my laptop on vacation, but because of the way it contributed to my meaningful story, I was able to embrace it. And I did everything I could to minimize the impact on my family by getting started before the sun rose.

Life is full of gray areas, and you will encounter them. But when you do, embrace them. Press into your Worthy Wins. If none of the obvious answers seem right, dig deeper. Step back and navigate those challenging moments in a way that aligns with the meaningful story that you want to be true of your life.

THE SWIRL OF SURVIVAL

Our pursuit of winning where it's worthy will always be challenged by the incessant demands of the urgent. An email in your inbox, a meeting to attend, a phone call to return, a presentation to build—the clock always feels like it's ticking in the background to get these urgent tasks done.

This is what I like to call the *swirl of survival*.

And we *all* live in it.

It's a reflection of our modern world—so much to do, but never enough time.

Endless distractions.

An ever-present pull of technology and the dopamine hit it offers us at any given moment.

Most days I find myself just trying to survive amidst everything that's going on, and I'm guessing you can relate.

We're all just doing our best.

The problem is, in the midst of the swirl, we're prone to get distracted from what's worthy. Peter Drucker, referred to by many as the "father of management," said this about leaders in his book *The Effective Executive*: "Without an action plan, the executive becomes a prisoner of events. And without check-ins to reexamine the plan as events unfold, the executive has no way of knowing which events really matter and which are only noise."[42]

This is true for us regular humans, too—not just executives. And I'm just as guilty as anyone. Too often, I'm a prisoner to the seemingly urgent events that are part of my everyday life.

About six months into life as a consultant, Erin asked me an important question: "How will you know if consulting is *not* working?"

It wasn't something I'd even considered prior to her question. I was so confident that it was going to work that I hadn't even gone down that road.

Her question started my gears spinning.

Obviously, if I stopped making money, that would show that it's not working.

But there was something deeper to consider. Making money wasn't the only thing that defined success for my consulting business.

It wasn't even the main thing.

Her question was timely. On the night she asked me, I had just returned from being gone sixteen of the previous thirty days. So I asked myself: If I had tons of clients and plenty of income, but I was traveling all the time, spending time away from my family, was my plan really working?

No. Not for me. That would not be a Worthy Win.

Did I need to make a living? Be strategic about my business? Dig deep and sacrifice to set myself up for success? Travel when necessary to be with clients? Yes, yes, yes, and yes. Those were all part of my new reality as a consultant.

But if being present to my family was a Worthy Win to me, then I had to recognize that I was at risk of building a business that wouldn't allow for it. I had gotten so swept away in the swirl of survival that I hadn't taken the time to step back and recognize that fact.

I'm so grateful for Erin's question. She snapped me out of my chase for clients and revenue and prompted me to pause and remember that I don't want to just win—I want to win where it's worthy.

I was in the swirl of survival, and it was a wake-up call that prompted me to reexamine my plan and make sure I was building my business with attention to the biggest priorities in my life.

If you realize that you've been swept up in the swirl of survival, the solution is simple: Press pause. Set aside intentional time in your schedule to stop, reflect, and assess whether you're going in the direction you want to go. Get clear on your priorities, what's really important to your life, and make sure your focus is directed toward those areas.

The swirl of survival is a constant. It's here, and it's not going anywhere. But if we're aware of it and we make intentional time to step outside of it, we can keep from getting stuck in the swirl as we pursue what's worthy.

DRIFT

You might remember that back in 2023, Ja Morant was a budding NBA superstar. Domination on the court. Tons of attention and love off of it. He was the next big thing.

But then he was suspended for an incident with a firearm on social media.

And then, that same year, he got suspended *again* for a similar incident.[43]

The sports world was shocked.

And so was I.

This wasn't the Ja Morant I had gotten to know through my work at Nike. A team of coworkers and I had been developing Ja's brand plan for the company, and *this* was not the brand or the plan anyone had in mind.

Less than three years before, we had a strategic planning meeting with him at the Ritz-Carlton in Marina Del Rey.

When Ja arrived with his dad, his uncle, and his agent, I was struck by how kind, soft-spoken, and humble this young NBA star was. He was happy to be there, excited about his future and the chance to work with Nike. During the meeting, Ja shared with us about the challenges he faced on his way to the NBA, about how he was often overlooked, and how that left a chip on his shoulder that he used to drive his performance on the court. His story of hard work and perseverance was incredible, and as we parted ways that day, there was so much optimism amongst our team about the special athlete in front of us.

So when the news broke about Ja's troubles a few short years later, I asked myself: How could he do something so foolish?

The truth is that I don't know Ja very well, and I haven't talked to him since any of these incidents, but my guess is that part of Ja's problem is that he hadn't defined what it meant to win in his life.

Drift happens—to *all* of us.

When there's no clear definition of winning in the short or long term, it becomes easy for any of us to drift off course.

And that's exactly what happened to Ja—after such a promising start to his career, he found himself in a place that was most definitely *not* on the path to winning.

When we don't have clarity on our Worthy Wins, it's easy to lose focus on our destination and drift. Over and over, I've had moments in my own life when I've done things that diverged from who I ultimately want to be. Whether it's a small choice, a poorly spoken word, or a moment when I lost my cool, I've been there.

I am prone to drift, just like Ja.

I believe we all are.

If, during that meeting three years ago, we had presented Ja's situation—the Instagram posts, the suspensions, the backlash he faced—as a hypothetical future scenario, there would have been a resounding "No way!" from everyone in the room, including Ja himself.

He absolutely did not *intend* to end up in the situation he found himself in.

And the good news for Ja is that those moments don't have to be the defining moments of his life or NBA career.

I'm still rooting for him.

I believe the young man we met in that conference room can turn the corner and have a story full of Worthy Wins.

And what's better news for all of us—including Ja—is that just because we're prone to drift doesn't mean we have to drift forever. If we take the time to get explicitly clear on what we want to be true at the end of our lives, we can get there. If we keep our eyes on our target, we can stay on course—or course correct when we've drifted.

ISOLATION

Last year, Erin and I traveled to Greece and Italy to celebrate our tenth wedding anniversary. While we were touring the famed Doge's Palace in Venice, I was struck by a *unique* lock-and-key structure.

There was a mailbox, but it was unlike any other I'd ever seen because it had three separate locks.

Why in the world would they need three keys to open one simple mailbox?

The mailbox was protecting people from themselves and protecting community members in turn. How so? Corruption was rampant in Venice at that time.

And the documents that went into these mailboxes were extremely important—with people's lives literally on the line.

So, the Venetians wanted to make sure that no single person or pair of people could get into the mailbox on their own. Three separate keys went to three separate people, and all three of those keys were required to open the lock. This created a system of accountability to shield from the corruption that was happening around the city, protecting any one of the three key owners from going it alone and making an unwise choice.

Today, we live in the most "connected" era ever.

We have access to people 24-7 through the internet and social media.

And yet, we are in the midst of a loneliness epidemic.

According to a 2023 report from the United States Surgeon General, we are more isolated than we've ever been. And we are so often relying on our phones for what passes as a connection to the people around us.[44] The report shows there are vast threats each of us faces as a result of loneliness and isolation. This false form of connection can easily lead us to a place of complete isolation, no matter how many "likes" we're getting on our posts or "friends" we have on digital platforms.

Personally, I've seen the consequences of isolation play out over and over again with people I know and love. When someone is tired, worn out, and frustrated, they are prone to make quick decisions in isolation in an attempt to relieve the pressure on their lives. I'm talking *huge* life decisions—substance abuse, divorce, career changes—that have major ramifications.

Making a life-altering decision
in isolation is *extremely* risky.

That's why, just like in Doge's palace, we have to protect ourselves from isolation. Especially when making big life decisions. These become pivotal moments with huge potential consequences. The kind of outcomes that are completely life-altering.

What I've seen with my friends in isolation is that they too often make blow-it-up-and-start-over kinds of decisions.

The types of decisions that should *never* be made alone, in a vacuum, or without clarity around how they fit into the pursuit of Worthy Wins.

In my life, I call these "three-lock decisions." If there are three locks, that means I need three unique keyholders (and I'm not one of them). I'm accountable to all three key holders in any major decision that I make.

It may look different for you, but my key holders are the following:

1   God (by inviting Him into my journey)
2   Erin (we're teammates on the journey together)
3   A trusted friend or multiple friends (it varies depending on the circumstances and expertise required)

In any big decision, I invite my three keyholders in, leaning on them for accountability and trusting their advice. They should only grant me the use of their key *after* we've landed with clarity on what my Worthy Wins are and which decision will lead me closer to them.

When we are alone, we are vulnerable.

More prone to drift.

More prone to make choices that aren't aligned with our Worthy Wins.

And more prone to walk down a path that doesn't lead where we said we wanted to be going.

We always need people around us who we trust, but especially when it comes to those three-lock decisions. Find people who you can lean on—the ones who will help you on your journey (just as you help them on theirs).

Life is not meant to be lived alone.

And big decisions are no different.

Prior to starting at Nike in 2012, my life was at a fork in the road, torn between a job offer and a hope of landing at Nike. Did I want to accept an executive director role at the United Way (and satisfy their request for a *minimum* five-year commitment)? Or did I want to keep pushing to see if a door would open up at Nike? The United Way opportunity was going to expire shortly, and after having a dialogue for more than a year with a vice president at Nike about a specific role that I was well qualified for, that door slammed shut. They had filled the role with someone else.

I was stuck.

Two friends, Chad and Kent, had an idea for me to try and get unstuck. They called it a "clearness committee." It was a new idea to me at the time, but in essence, it was an evening to bring together the people who knew me best to help me drill down into my deepest desires. Not to tell me what to do, but to sit me in the center of a circle and probe on what was most important to me. To allow me to ponder what really mattered to me. To help me unravel all the rivaling thoughts and work toward clarity. This was an in-person, real-time version of my three key holders coming together.

After I had withstood the hot seat, answered their questions, and processed my answers, I realized I didn't actually want to do the job at the United Way—regardless of the good the organization did for the community. The clearness committee helped me see that I wanted to confidently push forward and try to find an open door at Nike.

We are not meant to make these decisions and go through this journey on our own. In fact, the clearness committee was a picture of how life is supposed to be lived. In the book of Matthew, Jesus said, "Again, I tell you that if two of you on earth agree about anything you ask for, it will be done for you by my Father in heaven. For where two or three are gathered in my name, there am I among them."[45]

Jesus was encouraging us to come together and partner on figuring out the path forward. We live in a siloed world—or as the US surgeon general says, a lonely world. For most people I know, there is plenty of digital connection to others, but in most cases it has limited depth. The clearness committee is an example to break down the walls as we ponder the route ahead.

In his book *Heroic Leadership*, Chris Lowney shares a practice the Jesuits use to help one chart a course for the future. The process, which is inspired by the Spiritual Practices of Saint Ignatius, involves a "director" role—often played by, coaches, mentors, or parents. This director helps with the "mining" efforts "but acts in a way 'to point,' as with the finger, to the vein in the mine, and let each one dig for himself."[46]

Regardless of the exact medium, it's clear to me that we are not meant to do life's journey alone. We especially aren't meant to make massive, trajectory-altering decisions without clarity. The people who know me the best have been so crucial to me as I've come upon these moments. They have been the difference makers as I've sought to figure out what really matters to me.

They've protected me from myself and only provided the keys to the lock when I've really taken the time.

This chapter doesn't represent an exhaustive list of the tensions and pitfalls you'll face on the journey to win where it's worthy. But it's a good start.

The more aware we are of the potential pitfalls we might face, the better we'll be able to avoid them in our search for Worthy Wins.

REFLECTION QUESTIONS

- Are there areas you need to counterinvest in to be better prepared in heavy times in other areas?

- Is there a current or upcoming area in which you feel torn between two important things?

- In which areas of your life are you prone to get swept up into the Swirl of Survival?

- Are you clear enough on your Worthy Wins to avoid drifting off course?

- Who are your three key holders for the three-lock decisions in your life?

CHAPTER 10

THE SECRET FORMULA

THE FIRST TIME I ever met Kobe, he shared a truth about greatness that will stick with me forever.

We were at his office in Costa Mesa for a photo shoot. We needed to capture some photo and video content to support the launch of his first Protro shoe—the Kobe 1 Protro. During the visit, we carved out time to do an interview about the shoe and a few other topics.

In particular, we wanted to ask him about one of his biggest passions: greatness.

And we wanted his take on how someone becomes the greatest version of themselves.

His answer was important and very matter-of-fact: "Results come from the work you put in. There aren't any magic formulas or super elixirs that are going to get you to your dream. That only comes from hard work."

Mic drop.

Kobe's secret formula was that there are no secret formulas.

His secret to success was hard work.

But I learned over my time working with him that there was more to greatness for Kobe. Hard work wasn't the only key in Kobe's mind about how to become great. Anyone who ever knew or worked with Kobe would tell you that he had an *extreme* urgency about him.

He had no time for wasting time.

A year after that first photo shoot, Kobe was in Portland for an annual planning session for his work with Nike. As the session was drawing to a close, we began discussing the action items and next steps.

One of the most critical tasks was getting back down to his office in Costa Mesa for a working session. We needed to take ten people from Nike with us for the meeting, so it was a little bit of a logistical challenge to get the dates lined up that would work for all the parties involved. We told him we'd follow up with him in a few days about when we'd be able to come down and meet. All the words weren't even out of my mouth before I could tell that my response wasn't going to fly. Kobe quickly quipped back, "Let me guess—you're thinking a month from now?"

The tone of his question made his disdain about that timeline obvious to all of us in the room.

Was a month likely how long it would take to get three vice presidents and seven other teammates on planes to spend a full day in Southern California? Yes.

Was taking that long acceptable to Kobe? Nope.

That moment, amongst many others during my time working with him, revealed to me that Kobe *hated* wasting time.

Urgency was of the essence, always.

And that was a huge part of his approach to greatness.

Those two interactions—the first time meeting in Costa Mesa and then during his annual business session a year later—demonstrated something that I came to observe more in Kobe over time: While there was no magic to his greatness, he *did* have a secret formula.

The first two elements were urgency and consistency. He said himself that greatness came from consistent hard work. And he constantly had a sense of urgency about him, never content to sit around and waste time when he could be moving forward.

But there was a third element to Kobe's greatness formula.

And I would call this the *secret* part of the formula.

Kobe always said that he was chasing perfection.

That was his mountaintop. His target, so to speak.

But Kobe was fully aware that he wasn't going to reach that mountaintop in one day. Or one week.

Or one month.

Or even one year.

He knew that perfection was a *lifelong* journey.

Even if he also knew that he'd actually never reach perfection. But the only way to get close—and become the best version of himself—was to go after it and get better *today*.

And then repeat that day after day after day.

Kobe was incredibly wise in this way. And this demonstrated the secret element of his approach to greatness. The element that no one ever associated with him because his consistency and his urgency were so outspoken.

Patience.

It feels difficult to even write because Kobe was *not* patient—and yet he was at the same time. He had to be patient in order to chase perfection because time was the only thing that would allow that growth.

So for Kobe, it was about going on the journey every single day with urgency and consistency while also understanding that moving toward his destination was a process. Even though he didn't like waiting for anything, he knew that the only way to achieve what he wanted was to work hard over a very long period of time. And that took patience.

The Path to Greatness: Urgency + Consistency + Patience

That was Kobe's secret formula—the three elements that showed in his life as he chased perfection. He worked hard, but his focus was always on the journey.

Honestly, I don't like formulas. It was one of my hesitations around writing a book—when you write a book, people want you to tell them how to make magic happen. They want a magical formula. I know this because when I read a book, *I* want a magical formula.

But the reality is the only true "magic" formula is the one Kobe used.

Consistency in working toward your Worthy Wins.

Urgency to take advantage of every single opportunity.

And enough patience to focus on the journey, not the destination.

We won't ever "arrive" at our destination until our last breath. There are points in time when it may seem like everything comes together, but those aren't the destination—they're more like flight layovers. Your journey may feel like it's reached a destination, but really, it's just a one-time stop before life moves on.

When Jesus was asked which commandment was the greatest, He said, "You shall love the Lord your God with all your heart and with all your soul and with all your mind. This is the great and first commandment. And a second is like it: You shall love your neighbor as yourself."[47]

This was a big question, but Jesus didn't answer with a command that instructed people with how to get past the finish line. Instead, He answered with two things that He wanted us all to do *along the journey*.

And that journey isn't some monumental task. It's not the entire mountain that's in front of us.

The journey is *today*.

Then the next day.

Then the next.

Since there's no magic elixir, no super pill, it doesn't happen all in one moment. We just take one step, move forward, and then take the next step.

That's the challenge I want to leave you with as we close: The journey is today.

That's the way Kobe saw it. That's the way Jesus lived and taught. And it's true for all of us. Our journey will lead us to where we want to go, but pursuing Worthy Wins isn't ultimately about reaching our destination. It's about the journey, the choices we make today that lead us in the direction we want to go and toward the kind of people we want to be. It's a lifelong journey, but if you keep taking it—one day at a time, one step at a time, one decision at a time—it's the most worthwhile thing you'll ever do.

REFLECTION QUESTIONS

- Are you currently acting with urgency and consistency in pursuit of your Worthy Wins?

- Are you operating with patience to embrace the highs and lows of your journey?

- What is one thing you could start today and do every day that would be moving you toward your Worthy Wins?

CHAPTER 11

THE AWARD PODIUM

SO—WHAT MATTERS? I began the introduction with that question. And it's fitting we return to it one final time as we end our time together in this book.

But the context of that question gets sharpened when I specifically consider the end of my life.

When I think about taking my last breath, the same picture keeps coming into my head.

It's not me in a hospital bed having withered away.

It's not me outside a door waiting for God to decide my fate.

It's actually me, looking like a young version of me.

I'm standing on a podium, waiting for an award ceremony to start.

When I was a kid, several years before my mom passed away, I started running track and field and cross-country. One of the things I remember most about those years of running—aside from the painful pushes to get over the finish line—was that at the end of the meet or race, there would always be a podium.

The podium was the moment you were given an award for how you ran the race.

But the award on the podium was always given for a *specific* race or event.

Maybe it was the eight hundred meters, or the high jump, or a three-thousand-meter cross-country race for eight-year-olds. Regardless, on the podium, awards were given for your performance in a distinct event.

The cool thing was that, as a kid, you got to choose which event you competed in. But no one could do all the events. You *had to* make a choice.

What did you want to invest your time into?

What did you enjoy doing?

What did you want to get better at?

What were you built to have success at?

Some combination of answers to those questions led you to decide about what events to compete in.

Or, put differently, to make a declaration where you wanted to win.

Then it was on you to do the work to succeed at those specific events.

Ultimately, your training determined how you performed in the competition.

But if you had said you wanted to win at the ten-thousand-meter race and trained like someone who was going to run the hundred-meter dash, the likelihood of success at the ten-thousand-meter race was not going to be good.

The best chance of winning was to be clear about what you wanted to win at and then execute a strategic training plan to be successful at that *specific* event.

Because the winner of each event—the one who had made a declaration and prepared best to win that specific event—would stand atop the podium and get their award.

That's probably why this picture of me on a podium keeps coming into my head as I think about my death.

Not because I won a few running awards as a boy but because I know that, at the end of every race, there will always be a podium.

And just like when I was kid, I have the amazing opportunity to decide what I want to compete in.

More specifically, what do I want to try to win at?

And what will be worth all the effort it takes to succeed?

Because the picture in my head keeps reminding me that, at the end of my life, I will have competed at something. As I talked about in chapter 4, the apostle Paul uses this very same metaphor about a race as he compelled the people of Ephesus to run to be victorious. I'm challenged by that because it reminds me I'm going to stand on a proverbial podium and receive an award for all that I invested my life into.

Will it be the things that mattered most to me?

The things that were *worthy* of my limited TEA?

Or something else that is less worthy?

For the record, I'm not talking about earning salvation or approval from God. That's not what this award ceremony is about.

This is not about personal value or how much God loves me. Those things are already established—I have value, and I am immeasurably loved by God. This is not about God giving me an award for my life, though I do long for him to say, "Well done."

For me, the podium moment is a reminder that I have a choice about what event I want to compete in and that my success in that event will be determined by the way I invest my TEA day after day after day.

When I stand on that podium, having taken my last breath, I want to have competed and pursued winning at the things that actually mattered.

I want to win where it's worthy.

And I desire the same for you. I'm honored you've made it this far in the book, and I want to invite you to join me on this journey.

As a reminder, you don't have to quit your job.

This is not about a specific job per se.

This is about orientating your life toward what is truly worthy.

And taking steps now that you'll look back upon and say they were leading you toward your long-term Worthy Wins.

So when that proverbial podium moment comes, you will have clarity and peace about what you invested your TEA into.

That's what it means to win where it's worthy.

And you will be able to say, "*That* was worth it."

———

HERE ARE THREE ways you can explore getting started.

1 SELF-GUIDED

Go back to the end of chapters 3–9 and answer each of the reflection questions. What do you notice about your answers? How can you lean into them today?

Or, if you're looking for a simpler starting point—no page turning necessary—answer the four questions below right now, and remind yourself of your answers every day.

Remember: You can win almost anywhere, but you can't win everywhere. These specific questions require doing *less* and focusing on less rather than doing *more*. And the way you answer these questions will give you a clear focus on what it will mean for you to win where it's worthy.

- What are the characteristics that best represent the person you want to ultimately become by the end of your life?
- Who are the *specific* people that will matter most to you at the end of your life?
- What are the accomplishments that will matter most to you at the end of your life?
- What are the intentional desires and consistent actions (active intentions) needed to ensure that you win with each of those people and at each of those things?

2 TOOLS AND RESOURCES TO HELP

At my website, worthywins.co/book, you'll find a set of tools and resources that are available to assist you on your journey to get Worthy Wins.

3 SPEAKING AND CONSULTING

The questions, tools, and resources will help you get started and move forward in your journey, but I know hands-on guidance can be helpful as well. I have limited capacity for speaking and consulting work, but I love working directly with teams and people to help them pursue their own Worthy Wins. If you're interested in having me speak or consult for you or your organization, please reach out at john@worthywins.co.

ACKNOWLEDGMENTS

There have been a group of people who have propelled me on this journey. Without their support and pushing—I might still be sitting around dreaming about this book.

First and foremost, my wife, Erin—you have been a constant champion (and kick in the butt) for me on this book. You've sacrificed a lot of mornings so I could go and do the writing. Truly, I could not have written this book without you. Thank you and I love you!

Kent Hotaling—your faithfulness in my writing journey is unmatched. You've been reading and offering feedback on my writing for more than fifteen years. I'm eternally grateful for your influence on me, and both directly and indirectly on this book.

Jordan Rogers and Andy Pawlowski—you both pushed and encouraged me in different ways along my writing journey. But it was both of you who supported the power of the term Worthy Wins and convinced me to go with it. I appreciate you guys so much!

Cam Bray—your faithfulness as a friend and offering feedback on my writing—both before and during the actual book writing process—has put wind in my sails. I'm so grateful for you.

Shea Washington—you pushed me over the edge to finally take the leap and write this. I'm glad you decided to write that email challenging me to go for it.

OG Worthy Wins Newsletter readers—y'all have been with me from the beginning and your affirmation of the value of what I'm sharing has kept me going. Thank you!

Jon Gordon—thank you for your belief and encouragement. And for your reminder that Worthy Wins are worth it!

To my publishing team—So much gratitude for the team and their belief in this project. Thank you to Alex, Will, Donnel, Gin, Michael, Chloie, and the rest of the crew. Your support was a blessing to me!

Andrew Blackburn—last but not least, you have been such an amazing and patient partner to me in this writing process. You've pushed me forward and sharpened my thoughts in immeasurable ways. So very thankful for you!

ABOUT THE AUTHOR

John Olinger's journey from Nike marketing executive to purpose-driven leader began with a single question: What will matter *most* when I get to the end of my life? After spending a decade creating breakthrough campaigns for Nike and Jordan Brand—including three years leading Global Marketing for Kobe Bryant—an unexpected loss changed everything. Today, John combines his strategic marketing expertise with hard-won wisdom to help organizations and individuals win where it matters most. A follower of Jesus, he lives in Saint Augustine, Florida, with his wife Erin and their three energetic boys, where he serves as a strategic consultant, executive coach, and keynote speaker. Visit john-olinger.com to learn more about Worthy Wins.

ENDNOTES

1 Phil Knight, *Shoe Dog* (Simon and Schuster, 2016) 281.

2 Stanford Report, "'You've Got to Find What You Love,' Jobs Says," June 12, 2005, https://news.stanford.edu/stories/2005/06/youve-got-find-love-jobs-says.

3 Rollo May, Ernest Angel, Henri F. Ellenberger, *Existence: A New Dimension in Psychiatry and Psychology* (Simon and Schuster, 1958), 49.

4 https://www.dictionary.com/browse/worthy.

5 John Mark Comer, *Practicing the Way* (Waterbrook, 2024), 67.

6 https://hbr.org/2019/12/what-happens-when-your-career-becomes-your-whole-identity.

7 *All or Nothing: Arsenal*, episode 6.

8 Knight, *Shoe Dog*, 281.

9 Tony Robbins, "Ask Better Questions," *Tony Robbins Blog*, accessed December 4, 2024, https://www.tonyrobbins.com/blog/ask-better-questions

10 Robert J. Waldinger and Marc Schulz, *The Good Life: Lessons from the World's Longest Scientific Study of Happiness* (Simon and Schuster, 2023), 30.

11 Matthew 4:18–22 (ESV).

12 1 Corinthians 9:24 (ESV).

13 Elon Musk (@elonmusk), "Unregretted user-minutes is the metric that matters most," December 13, 2022, https://x.com/elonmusk/status/1602804829583118341; "We're trying hard to make your feed as compelling as possible (maximize unregretted user minutes). How is it now vs 6 months ago?" May 7, 2023, https://x.com/elonmusk/status/1655257960002486273.

14 Waldinger and Schulz, *The Good Life*, 29.

15 Romans 12:2 (ESV).

16 Cal Newport, *Deep Work: Rules for Focused Success in a Distracted World* (Grand Central Publishing, 2016).

17 Andrew Huberman, "The Ideal Length of Time for Focused Work," posted September 10, 2022, by Huberman Lab Clips, YouTube, https://youtu.be/5HINgMMTzPE.

18 Luke 14:28–30.

19 John Doerr, *Measure What Matters* (Portfolio, 2018), 19.

20 Data Commons, "Life Expectancy Person," https://datacommons.org/tools/timeline#&place=country/USA&statsVar=LifeExpectancy_Person.

21 Ryan Ermey, "Warren Buffett's Advice for Avoiding Major Mistakes: 'Write Your Obituary and Figure Out How to Live Up to It,'" CNBC.com, May 8, 2023, https://www.cnbc.com/2023/05/08/warren-buffett-to-avoid-major-mistakes-write-your-obituary.html.

22 Donald Miller, *Hero on a Mission* (HarperCollins Leadership, 2022), xi.

23 Comer, *Practicing the Way*, 97.

24 Justin Kendrick, *Bury Your Ordinary: Practical Habits of a Heart Fully Alive* (David C. Cook, 2021), narrated by Justin Kendrick, at 43 min., 25 sec.

25 Luke 19:5–6 (ESV).

26 Viktor E. Frankl, *Man's Search for Meaning* (Beacon Press, 2006), 85.

27   Bob P. Buford, *Halftime: Moving from Success to Significance* (Zondervan, 2015), 98.

28   Miller, *Hero on a Mission*, 52.

29   Romans 9:3–5 (ESV).

30   Tim Schurrer, *The Secret Society of Success* (Thomas Nelson, 2022), 35.

31   Philippians 1:9–11 (ESV).

32   Robert McKee, *Story: Substance, Structure, Style, and the Principles of Screenwriting* (ReganBooks, 1997), 210.

33   Arthur C. Brooks and Oprah Winfrey, *Build the Life You Want* (Portfolio, 2023), 23.

34   Brooks and Winfrey, *Build the Life You Want*, 11.

35   Frankl, *Man's Search For Meaning*, 76.

36   Waldinger and Shultz, *The Good Life*, 184.

37   Doerr, *Measure What Matters*, 124.

38   Giada Di Stefano, Francesca Gino, Gary Pisano and Bradley Staats, "Learning By Thinking: How Reflection Improves Performance," https://papers.ssrn.com/sol3/papers.cfm?abstract_id=2414478.

39   Tim Schurrer, *The Secret Society of Success*, 23.

40   Schurrer, *The Secret Society of Success*, 23.

41   Kobe Bryant, *The Mamba Mentality: How I Play* (MCD, 2018), 33.

42   Peter Drucker, *The Effective Executive* (Collins, 2002), 13.

43   NBA.com New Service, "Ja Morant suspended 25 games by NBA," NBA.com, updated on June 16, 2023, https://www.nba.com/news/ja-morant-suspended-25-games.

44   Dr. Vivek H. Murthy, *Our Epidemic of Loneliness and Isolation: The US Surgeon General's Advisory on the Healing Effects of Social Connection and Community*, https://www.hhs.gov/sites/default/files/surgeon-general-social-connection-advisory.pdf

45 Matthew 18:19–20 (ESV).

46 Chris Lowney, *Heroic Leadership: Best Practices from a 450-Year-Old Company That Changed the World* (Loyola Press, 2005), 97.

47 Matthew 22:37–39 (ESV).